SELF-PUBLISH & SUCCEED

THE 'NO BORING BOOKS' WAY TO WRITE A NON-FICTION BOOK THAT SELLS

Stick Horse Publishing

Las Vegas, NV

Stick Horse Publishing
10845 Griffith Peak Dr #2
Las Vegas, NV 89135

ISBN: 978-1-7360315-0-6 (print)
ISBN: 978-1-7360315-1-3 (ebook)
ISBN: 978-1-7360315-2-0 (audiobook)

Ordering Information:
Special discounts are available on quantity purchases by corporations, associations, and others. For details, visit: juliebroad.com or call: email team@booklaunchers.com, or call 1-877-207-7666 x1

Publisher's Cataloging-in-Publication Data
Names: Broad, Julie, 1977- .
Title: Self-publish and succeed : the no boring books way to write a non-fiction book that sells /
    Julie Broad.
Description: Las Vegas, NV : Stick Horse Publishing, 2023.
Identifiers: ISBN 9781736031506 (pbk.) | ISBN 9781736031513 (ebook)
Subjects: LCSH: Authorship -- Handbooks, manuals, etc. | Creative nonfiction – Authorship. | Self
    -publishing -- Handbooks, manuals, etc. | BISAC: LANGUAGE ARTS & DISCIPLINES / Writing /
    Authorship. | LANGUAGE ARTS & DISCIPLINES / Writing / Business Aspects. | LANGUAGE
    ARTS & DISCIPLINES / Writing / Nonfiction.
Classification: LCC PN171.C74 B76 2023 | DDC 808.2 B--dc23

SELF-PUBLISH & SUCCEED

THE 'NO BORING BOOKS' WAY TO WRITE A NON-FICTION BOOK THAT SELLS

JULIE BROAD

To every author brave enough to not be boring.

TABLE OF CONTENTS

INTRODUCTION

Have you said you're going to write a book for months, maybe even years?

Perhaps, you're stuck wondering if your idea is any good. Possibly you're worried about whether it will make any money. Or maybe you've been trying to get a book deal based on a concept or a proposal but nothing has happened.

It would be easy to say that if you write a great book, publishers and readers will want it, but that isn't true. Many books, even good books, don't sell. Book deals worth signing are extremely rare (more on that in the first chapter). And, even then, it's impossible to be certain that your book will sell hundreds of copies, let alone thousands.

You've probably heard that the average nonfiction author sells fewer than 250 copies of their book.[1] It may even be lower when you factor in self-published books. In any case, there are three things you should know:

- The typical nonfiction book focuses on the author, not the reader, and that sets up the book (and author) for massive marketing challenges right from the start.

---

1   BJ Gallagher, "The Ten Awful Truths – and the Ten Wonderful Truths – About Book Publishing," *HuffPost*, updated December 6, 2017, https://www.huffpost.com/entry/book-publishing_b_1394159.

- A large percentage of nonfiction books are really boring because they lack a benefit driven hook and storytelling techniques, even if they contain great information.
- Many authors, especially self-published authors, don't plan for success; they write their book and hope it will sell.

Being mediocre is a choice. You are about to uncover our #noboringbooks process, which is about being awesome not average. You can (and should!) be an author of a book of which you'll be proud for the rest of your life. And, done right, your book will open doors to new experiences, opportunities, and connections.

Your book can make a difference in your life—and the life of your reader. I'm not going to provide you a secret way to successfully publish a book in 10 hours or offer you any gimmicks that will make your book an (almost meaningless) Amazon Bestseller. If you want to write, publish, and launch a book in 30 days, this is not your guide.

This is about creating something meaningful, and that takes effort and resources. Writing a book that has impact and that will change lives is a big project. Prepare to invest in this process. It's not overnight but it's worth it.

I know from experience that you will never regret writing your book if you do it right—but you will regret not doing it. Let's not waste another minute, okay? It's time to change your life and the life of your reader.

CHAPTER 1:

THE LIFE CHANGING BOOK

I was catching up with my coworker at Kimberly Clark Canada's Vancouver office on a Monday morning. We chatted about our weekends and shared a little office gossip.

It was like every casual conversation we'd ever had, except this one changed the course of my entire life.

My colleague, Lorna, a 20-plus-year veteran at the company, mentioned a book her daughter read. She said, *"You have so much more potential than just working here for your whole life.... Read it!"*

After work that day, I stopped at the bookstore (that's where you bought books in 2001) and picked up a copy of *Rich Dad Poor Dad: What the Rich Teach Their Kids About Money—That the Poor and Middle Class Do Not!* by Robert T. Kiyosaki and Sharon L. Lechter.

That night, I couldn't put it down. It forced me to begin to look at my life differently.

I grew up in rural Alberta, Canada, where my parents owned and operated a 20-room motel on the side of a highway.

They were always home for us as kids (we lived in a house attached to the motel), and after some tough years in the early '80s, they made a decent income. The problem was they were tied to this business 24/7. When the doorbell rang at 2:00 a.m., my dad put on his blue velvet housecoat and answered the door to rent someone a room. If one of the cleaning staff didn't show up for work, my parents had 20 toilets to clean. The business relied on them heavily.

It wasn't an easy place to be a kid because there were a lot of rules to keep us safe and not disturb the guests. At the same time, it fostered my entrepreneurial spirit.

I loved being a part of the business and collecting $7 an hour to do my work. It was fun to organize the cleaning staff lists and review which rooms were booked and which weren't. I always saw myself as owning my own business someday.

As I read *Rich Dad Poor Dad*, I realized my parents had created a good business for their family, but they didn't have financial freedom. They had jobs.

The book didn't change my long-term plan to get an MBA, earn a six-figure income, and eventually start my own business. But thanks to Robert Kiyosaki, I had a new mission:

To find a way to get my money working hard for me so I didn't always have to work hard for my money.

Stock investing seemed like gambling. I couldn't think of a brick-and-mortar business that could operate without me while I went back to school. But I could invest in real estate.

I started by reading everything written by best-selling author and investment advisor Robert G. Allen and just kept going. Every night I was reading, highlighting, and making notes in all the real estate investing books I could find.

After a few months and about 30 books, I hatched my plan and called it "Freedom 35." My goal was to secure financial freedom by age 35 and not need to work for someone else.

Like most things in life, it didn't work out quite the way I'd planned... but maybe it worked out even better than I could have imagined. I quit my six-figure job at the age of 30 and began raising capital to buy a rental house every month, and in 2009, together with my husband, launched a real estate training and education company.

When my husband detoured and got into acting, we decided to wrap up the business in 2016 and used the real estate to fund the greatest adventure of our lives as we moved to the US and I started Book Launchers. This incredible journey all began with *Rich Dad Poor Dad*. And it was the first of two books that completely changed my life. I'll tell you about the second book next. What I want you to know now is that it's entirely possible your book will change someone's life too.

And if you're thinking you need an agented book deal to get started, keep in mind that *Rich Dad Poor Dad* started off as a self-published book. Kiyosaki sold it anywhere he could, including in a chain of car washes in Texas.

THE BOOK DEAL YOU DON'T NEED

Being rejected by a traditional publisher was the best thing that could have happened to me, though it didn't feel like it at the time.

It was 2011. I'd been connected with a couple of different publishers about writing a book and I was really excited. I'd always wanted to write a book and after a decade of real estate investing, I had stories that I thought would make a great book.

My exchange with Wiley got serious but they weren't interested in my real estate book idea—they thought it was too general. They had a different spin on the topic of real estate and invited me to write a proposal to author that book.

I wrote the book proposal, hired people to review it, and sent it over. The editor at Wiley asked for some revisions and updates. We went back and forth a few times. When the proposal was finalized, I thought the only thing left was signing the contract.

The way it had gone I didn't think there was a question of whether I would get a book deal, it was a question of exactly when and what the terms were going to be.

Imagine my surprise when I received their rejection, which was simple and straightforward: *"The marketing department doesn't think you have a strong enough platform to sell books."*

They didn't reject the book. They rejected me.

I cried big, ugly, toddler-style tears for almost 20 minutes. I felt angry and hurt for months. But, ultimately, I am thrilled with what happened.

The desire to write a book ran deep for me. I also believed that the original book idea I had proposed was a book that needed to be written. I'd always regret it if I didn't write it. When I looked at my choices, giving up was not an option.

So I self-published.

I also proved the Wiley marketing department wrong. *More than Cashflow: The Real Risks and Rewards of Profitable Real Estate Investing* topped the charts of Amazon ranking ahead of Dan Brown and *A Game of Thrones* series selling thousands of print copies in its launch week. It turns out I could sell books, and I could sell a lot of them.

SELF-PUBLISHING IS MAINSTREAM...
YOU JUST MAY NOT KNOW IT

What do *The Toilet Paper Entrepreneur, Rich Dad Poor Dad, Will It Fly?* and *Choose Yourself!* have in common?

These are all best-selling, self-published books. In the case of *Choose Yourself!* by James Altucher, which reportedly has sold more than 100,000 copies,[2] and *Will it Fly?* by Pat Flynn, which hit *The Wall Street Journal's* Bestsellers list,[3] the authors didn't want traditional publishing deals. With *The Toilet Paper Entrepreneur* by Mike Michalowicz, the author self-published first and later chose to move to a traditional publishing house.[4]

What's most important to note is that there's no right or wrong way to publish your book. It's up to you to create success. Each of these authors is a well-known name today, not because they got a book deal but because they invested in writing a book that readers needed and made sure those readers knew their book existed.

The book may be about you but it's not for you.

Imagine you wrote a book that prevented someone from committing suicide, taught them how to get out of crippling debt, or helped them save their marriage from falling apart? Isn't that book a success, regardless of whatever else happens?

When you truly believe you have an obligation to help transform lives, you can focus on your writing to achieve that as the most important priority.

---

2   James Altucher, "How To Self-Publish A Bestseller: Publishing 3.0," TechCrunch, July 20, 2013, https://techcrunch.com/2013/07/20/how-to-self-publish-a-bestseller-publishing-3-0/.

3   Pat Flynn Instagram post, February 11, 2016, accessed September 8, 2020, https://www.instagram.com/p/BBqPwTwyOuf/?igshid=17t11t8ol8rc4.

4   Michalowicz, Mike, *Clockwork: Design Your Business to Run Itself,* Barnes & Noble, accessed September 8, 2020, https://www.barnesandnoble.com/w/clockwork-mike-michalowicz/1127681221.

What about the pursuit of bestseller status? While common, that approach is fundamentally flawed. **By focusing on fame and money, the author actually becomes the product, not the book.** You'll know you're thinking that way if you're wondering how you'll look to your friends, what you'll do if you sell thousands of copies (or don't!), and what other people will say about your writing.

When the book is the product, however, you can focus on telling a story and delivering a message that serves your audience in the best way possible—with the most compelling narrative, the most revealing examples, and the secrets only you can share for there to be results. You'll focus on creating a successful outcome for the reader, not for you.

The strong desire to be "chosen" is why many authors think they need a traditional publisher. Some also wrongly assume that publishers do all the marketing. If they thought more logically, they'd see that they were better off self-publishing. They would make more money—a lot more money—and keep the rights to their material!

Intellectual property is an enormous asset, and when you sign a traditionally published deal, you are giving it to someone else.

And here's the thing: You cannot control what ultimately happens after you publish your book unless you have a huge bankroll and can buy the result (which some authors do!). *What you can control is the effort and the intention behind the book.*

I'm not saying it's easy to set your ego aside. I was lucky in a way because Wiley crushed my ego and forced me to write the book that needed to be written, not the one they told me would sell. I was still scared nobody would buy my book, but I believed deeply that if I could help just one investor avoid my mistakes, it was worth it.

If you can set your ego aside and focus on the reader who needs you, the book will come from a much more emotionally stable place. And, if your book doesn't sell thousands of copies, you can more rationally evaluate the situation because your book was the product, not you.

Maybe traditional publishing is right for you; but quite likely, it's not.

The biggest benefits of pursuing a traditional deal is that the publisher pays the upfront costs and your book more easily gains traditional distribution. *The New York Times* is also more likely to deem your book worthy of their bestseller list if you hit big enough sales numbers. For the most part, you'll still be responsible for marketing. Your publisher may line up a few media appearances and book signings. Ultimately, though, the publisher is going to look at you to sell your book.

Let me repeat that part because it's important:

Even with a traditional publishing deal, the vast majority of authors are responsible for marketing their books.

In other words, you do all the sales work, and they take 75–85 percent of the revenue.[5] On a per book copy, traditionally published authors generally make less than $1 per book sold. In contrast, when they self-publish and sell through traditional channels like Amazon and bookstores, they make somewhere between $4–$6 per copy, depending on their price point, book size, and other print and publishing choices. When they sell books in bulk or direct, they can make two to three times that! So can you.

After five years, I did the math around what I made from the sale of my first book, *More than Cashflow: The Real Risks and Rewards of Profitable Real Estate Investing*. At the time, I earned $68,000 from the sale of books through Amazon, Kindle, bookstores, and libraries (not including the more than 1,000 books sold in bulk deals). On

---

5 Glen Yeffeth, "Are Royalties Fair? A Publisher Weighs In," Literary Agent Mark Gottlieb, accessed September 8, 2020, https://literaryagentmarkgottlieb.com/blog/are-royalties-fair-a-publisher-weighs-in.

retail sales alone, if I had a traditional publishing deal, I would have made $8,892—more than 80 percent less.

Very few authors will get the opportunity to be traditionally published,[6] even if they want to be. Publishers often want "sure things," which means most authors need to have a level of fame, the right contacts, or an established publishing track record to land a deal.

In exchange for working with them, you're more likely to find yourself offered a "hybrid" contract, which involves your footing some, or all, of the upfront costs and giving up a chunk of the royalty payments.

What does this mean? Put bluntly, you take all the risk, still have to do all the work (or almost all the work) to write and market your book and then, if you succeed, give some of your profits to someone else.

There are some advantages to the hybrid publishing arrangement. It brings a professional team to the table to do the work of editing and designing your book. They have distribution channels. And they usually don't own the rights or control your content.

For me, though, control is important.

It's my intellectual property, and I want to own it. If it does well, I want to be the one to benefit.

When it comes to your book, if someone in Bulgaria wants to license the rights, you probably want control over the choice to do that, or not. If a TV producer wants to turn your story into a film or a television series, you will want to be at the helm of that discussion as well.

Writing a book that matters is going to be a lot of work, no matter which route you take to publish your book. **You don't need to be "chosen" to have an impact on a reader.** Plus, your book can be

---

6   "What are the odds of getting a book deal?" Jericho Writers, accessed September 8, 2020, https://jerichowriters.com/hub/get-published/getting-a-publishing-deal/.

high quality and popular just as easily as it can flop, whether you self-publish or not. In fact, sometimes a traditionally published author thinks their success is so guaranteed they don't hustle as much as a self-published author.

The bottom line: If you invest in the same kind of experienced team as a traditional publisher would hire and if your book is well thought out and looks professional, consumers won't care how your book was published. They won't even know.

What they care about are things we'll cover in upcoming chapters—the hook, endorsements, testimonials, and ultimately, what your book will do to help readers in their lives right now.

GO AHEAD...GIVE YOUR BOOK THE HOOK

The buried treasure. The pot of gold at the end of the rainbow. The golden ticket. It's all right here at the start of Chapter 2. You don't have to read 10 chapters or follow some 30-day program on my website to get to it.

The single most important thing you need to write a great book is:

A HOOK!

If your book has a great hook, it is much more likely to sell well, and it might change your life forever.

Even cooler, if you get your hook right, you'll be clear on who your ideal reader is and the impact your book will have on their life. You'll know the problem they have and how you are going to solve it—in a way that nobody else is helping them solve it right now.

This makes it easy for a reader to see why they need your book, and it makes it ultra-easy for people to share your book with others because they can clearly say why someone should read it.

NO MORE BORING BOOKS

In film, the hook is the "logline," the brief (often one sentence) summary that piques someone's interest in the story.

It's the single thread that ties your book together, creates curiosity, and sells the work.

In nonfiction, it needs to answer an essential question: what's in it for the reader?

What is the outcome you want for your reader when they are done reading your book?

Too many authors sit down and start writing without thinking about the fundamental point of their book.

When you do this, you'll also quickly realize that you need complete clarity about your ideal reader. If you don't know your ideal reader, then your hook will be weak, if it exists at all.

One of the most common things I hear is, "I want the reader to feel inspired."

Guess what? Inspiration has massive value, but it's also very general. How is your book going to make the life of your reader better or different in real, concrete ways?

If you don't know who your reader is, you're facing your first challenge. Pull out your to-do list and write READER RESEARCH at the top.

HOW TO BECOME A MIND READER

The best books allow readers to visualize themselves in any given situation—to see solutions, experience change, and be inspired to action. That doesn't happen if your book is boring, and it also does NOT happen if you don't know how to get into the minds of your readers and meet them right where they are today. If you don't know the hopes, dreams, obstacles, and fears of your ideal readers, then you need to spend some time getting to know them.

First, please allow me to tell you who your ideal reader is not…
It's not everyone.

EVERYBODY is not your audience. No one has that audience.

Your ideal reader is specific.

There are always people who won't be your audience. Health conscious folks like myself won't drink Coke or Pepsi, no matter how many "feel good" commercials they produce or how many coupons they offer. We all need to see a doctor from time to time, but we each look for something different in our medical care professionals. And while we all have eyes, some of us may want to have surgery while others are content with contacts and still others choose to wear eyeglasses.

We may have universal needs but we fulfill them in different ways.

Forget the idea that your book is for everyone.

I once heard someone say, "My book is for everyone with a paycheck."

I laughed and asked, "Do you think your book is for me?"

He said, "No, you run your business."

"Yes, and I also get a paycheck from it," I said, then added, "Is your book for everyone working at McDonald's or In-N-Out Burger?"

"Sure, if they want to move up," he replied. That was the key! His book wasn't for anyone with a paycheck. It was for people working in entry-level or low-paying jobs who wanted to grow their career. I dug even deeper, and it turned out his book was specifically for people working in Fortune 500 companies with clear hierarchies and career paths. His book would teach readers how to navigate those paths and accelerate their rise in their organization.

Second, your ideal reader is not a demographic, for goodness' sake!

Maybe the demographic is *part* of what constitutes your audience. Perhaps, you are focusing your book on women or men or nonbinary individuals, but there's a lot more to it than that.

For instance, author Alec Hanson published a book called *Bypassed*. It's for mortgage professionals who are getting left behind by the digital consumer.

Alec could have said, "My ideal reader is a mortgage professional." He might have argued that everyone in the mortgage business will benefit from what he's teaching in the book. Online marketing is a must when it comes to strategies that will attract new clients and build a mortgage business.

But that's not specific enough, and writing to "every mortgage professional" would result in a book that isn't clear enough to get into the mind of the reader. His book, it turned out, is specifically for mortgage professionals getting left behind by technology. These people are likely to have been in the industry for a while and are used to building businesses based on referrals. They are the people who built websites 10 years ago and haven't updated them. They have Facebook but don't use it for business. You can't find them online when you search your local market for a mortgage professional. These professionals have never livestreamed on any sort of video platform.

Alec's ideal reader isn't someone like him— he's tech savvy. He livestreamed his book unboxing and live streams regularly on many platforms. He's done intense research into the industry and knows who needs his help. As a result, he knows his ideal reader's mindset, fears, hopes, and can speak directly to those in his book.

If you don't have your audience nailed down, what can you do?

1. Consider your ideal client for your business. If you're writing a book associated with your business, then it makes sense to write a book that is perfectly positioned to appeal to your ideal client or customer.

2. If you are branching away from your current career or business, you can offer your process or solution in the form of one-on-one coaching to a selection of people. *Spending time with people offering your solution, service, and guidance will help* you see what problems people really need help with and what you say and offer that has a big impact.

3. Conduct "Avatar Interviews" with people you think are your ideal readers to get to know them and their interests better. (If you've never done Avatar Interviews listen to the podcasts Alex Charfen has released on the subject—his process is the best I've seen).

4. Visit online forums and Facebook or LinkedIn groups to locate your ideal reader and follow their discussions. Check out Quora.com for questions and answers to understand what your ideal reader thinks and values and to find other recommended resources.

5. Search books that will compete with your book and read the reviews on Amazon and Goodreads. Read what people like but also focus on what they don't like. What do they want that is a bit different and missing from existing books? I'm not looking for haters; I'm looking for people who provide constructive ideas. For example, while doing research for a client writing a book on handling cancer treatments, I noticed a competing book had several comments that said the book was great but neglected the emotional aspect of dealing with cancer. This helped us advise her that there was an opportunity to position her book with more of an emotional component.

When you get your ideal reader right, you can speak to where they are in their life right now. You know the solutions they have already tried to solve their problem or achieve their desired result. The problems are clear to you. You're also able to perfectly position your book as the thing they need right now and why your approach is different than everything they have tried before. This makes you seem like you can read their mind.

If you can present your solution in a way that allows your readers to see it as the solution *they* need, you'll stand out to your reader. You'll also become the obvious choice for anyone who deals with that issue and needs to refer other people to a solution too!

A READER FOCUSED HOOK

It can be hard to see what is cool about your book idea when you're working on it alone. If you haven't already, take a good look at other, similar books in your industry. Ask yourself:

- What is the common theme?
- What is different about your idea?
- What have you experienced that runs counter to conventional wisdom?
- What is the problem you'll solve?
- How do you solve it in a way that others haven't?

If you're still struggling, think about something that really frustrates you or even makes you mad about your industry. What do you wish everyone knew so they could avoid pain or get better results faster?

For example, one thing that drove me crazy as a real estate investor and coach was the belief that real estate was a passive investment. When I believed that, I ended up with a property manager who robbed rent money from me, and my husband and I wound up the not-so-proud owners of a known crack house. It's an active business and believing otherwise results in problems.

The hook to my first book, *More than Cashflow*, was written to address the ideas that people had about real estate that were false or incredibly misleading based on my personal experience.

Figure that out for your business or industry and you'll find the hook.

The hook tells readers why they should invest time and money in you and your book. It might be in the subtitle of your book but it doesn't have to be. When you talk about your book, this is what you will say to get them excited about reading it.

One of our clients wanted to write a book on everything he'd learned about horror movies and books. He'd hosted a popular podcast on horror for a few years. How do you find a hook about the history of horror as a genre? A book about evaluating the horror genre didn't seem to have wide appeal, but what happened is a really cool story.

Author S. A. Bradley spent some time with our Story Expert, and they came up with a hook that had a unique twist revealed in the title:

Screaming for Pleasure: How Horror Makes You Happy and Healthy.

The book explores everything there is to know about the greatest horror movies and books, why experiencing horror is so important for so many people, and how horror can help you get in touch with parts of yourself that you have tried to hide. S.A. Bradley, the author, even found research that backed up his premise and showed that getting scared provides health benefits.

"Audiences love to be scared but behind every muffled scream is something deeper and even more fascinating," he wrote.

Another author, Michael Brenner, came to us with a concept he was about to toss in the trash: The importance of empathy in business. He initially titled his book *The Empathy Formula*. He had some really good material, but early readers of his draft manuscript were not kind, suggesting it needed a ton of help. He didn't know how to save it, but he'd put a ton of work into it so he asked us if there was hope.

The book was missing that juicy "what's in it for the reader" hook. Empathy lacked the marketing appeal that a book like his needed. Working with our team, discussing why he wrote the book, what the message really was intended to do for a reader, and having some fun with the subject matter, he blurted out, "Mean people suck, and they don't have to be mean to get results." That conversation led Michael to refocus the book, and *Mean People Suck: How Empathy Leads to Bigger Profits and a Better Life* was born. With a clear hook in the subtitle, he was able to position his book on empathy for great results!

TIME TO PITCH IT...OVER AND OVER

Once people know that you've written a book, you'll get asked a million times, "Hey, what's your book about?" Most who ask this are only half-heartedly interested so you have about 10 seconds before they totally tune out.

That means you have to practice and master what's called an "elevator pitch." It should be no more than two sentences. It's essentially your hook and what's in it for the reader.

If you can get your hook into the subtitle of your book, that's ideal. Then, you just have to say the title of your book, with the subtitle being your pitch, and you're good to go.

Rich Dad Poor Dad is probably the best example I've ever seen of this. He took four words and turned them into a phrase that will always be synonymous with his brand. The fact that his Rich Dad[7] is

---

7   While Robert Kiyosaki hasn't acknowledged this as fact, and still continues to let the myth of the "Rich Dad" exist, Keith Cunningham was Robert Kiyosaki's business partner prior to *Rich Dad Poor Dad* and is the original creator of a large portion of the concepts attributed to "Rich Dad" in the book. When I learned this, I felt like I was a kid discovering Santa wasn't real. It was devastating, and yet, doesn't change the power of this book as an example of so many things that were done right.

fictional doesn't take away from the power of what he has built from a single book and a powerful hook. His subtitle says it all:

What the Rich Teach Their Kids About Money—That the Poor and Middle Class Do Not.

It's a little long as far as subtitles go but there's not a person, rich or poor, who doesn't want to know that information. It sells the book with a curiosity-driven hook that promises a reward. All you need to do is tell people that subtitle and they will want to read the book.

The key is to get yours down to a sentence or two. You never know who may ask about your book. Maybe it's the owner of a bookstore chain, a book critic, a movie producer looking for the next big concept, or someone who has never read a book like yours. No matter who it is, the pitch is important. Your goal is to get people to say, *"Wow, I NEED to read that!"* or *"That sounds interesting, where can I buy it?"*

Or, if they don't say that, hopefully they say, "I have to tell my mom/best friend/boss about that book. They will love it!"

Have it memorized to the point that you can recite it in your sleep. If you're startled in the middle of the night by a ghost that pops out from under your bed and asks, "What's your book about?" you should immediately be able to deliver your pitch before you scream in terror.

A NEW PERSPECTIVE ON DAYS THAT SUCK

When you haven't experienced struggle, pain, fear, or deep hurt, it's difficult to write a book. If you haven't tried and failed, you don't really have lessons to share. Learning doesn't come from success. Learning comes from making mistakes and things going wrong.

One of the few clients I have had to let go in the middle of a book project was someone who struggled from day one to find a hook.

The client wrote about a topic in which he was interested but not experienced. Even after some editing, the book felt flat. It didn't feel real. The only good advice he offered came from things he'd read or courses he'd taken. The author hadn't established his own voice or authority, and nothing about the book made it a "must read."

The biggest source of the problem?

He grew up in a good home with means, had a great social circle, married the girl of his dreams, worked in his family business, and started making money through investments. Nothing had gone wrong.

I basically had to tell him that we weren't going to be able to continue working with him on that book: "The bad news is, we haven't been able to find a way to make this book connect with the audience you want to reach because you haven't had enough hard lessons learned in these areas. The good news is, you've had a really blessed life." I was relieved and surprised when he agreed and decided to abandon the project.

This author could have saved his book by interviewing people with stories about his subject, doing deep research of books covering the subject, and developing a unique perspective, with concrete examples, based on all of that work. That wasn't something he wanted to do though.

So take heart. If you've had a lot of challenges in your life, you likely have a great book in you. The best source of your hook is likely related to a defining moment in your life—and a defining moment, one worth celebrating because it gives you wisdom, is never one that starts out with good news.

STORIES GET ENERGY FROM THE NEGATIVE

Next time you're watching a really good movie, notice the best scenes are those that have a change in emotional value. For example, a happy couple has coffee together. Everything is going well until the woman receives a text message from an ex-boyfriend. The new boyfriend gets jealous and mad. He accuses her of leading on her ex. She gets up and leaves.

When I tell the story of writing my first book, *More than Cashflow*, people don't relate the fact that my book sold thousands of copies in the first week and went to #1 overall on Amazon. They relate to the deep, personal rejection I felt when the publisher said that they didn't think my platform was good enough to sell any books.

Even if you've never wanted to be published, you've been rejected. That's an emotion we can almost universally relate to. If I left out that part of the story, it would be fluffy and not at all interesting.

Bad things happen in business. There are challenges. Your story gets energy from the negative so you must include it in the stories you tell, especially in business settings.

You may prefer to focus on your successes and the good things in your life but that's boring. It's also not easy to relate to. We all have tough days. In fact, for many people, more things are usually going wrong than right.

Regardless of your ultimate message and promised outcome for the reader, be real about the journey to get there.

This is good news. It means that all those really tough days paid off. When you get through a difficult time, you learn lessons and have an incredible story to tell. And it just might be part of the hook of your book!

IF YOU WERE GOING TO DIE TOMORROW

Coming up with a hook can be challenging. You may know you want to write a book but you're not sure what it should be about.

Here's one way to narrow your focus:

Imagine you were going to die tomorrow. (It's a dark thought, but please play along—it's an important exercise.)

Take a moment to really consider it. Now imagine you've been invited to give a talk today. This will be your last talk ever.

What's your important message? What will benefit others? What have you learned that will change someone's life?

The hook of your book is in your answers to those questions!

My friend, Philip McKernan, an author, filmmaker, and keynote speaker, has built an entire series of events around this very concept, called "One Last Talk," and I share this idea because I want you to realize that the very thing that makes you and your book unique is YOU. Certainly, your professional experience and guidance (including things like "How-To" steps) are important and will be appreciated, but they are not going to be that different from other people in your business. The stuff that makes your book memorable, awesome, and unlike any other book on the market are the specific, personal stories that you would share if tomorrow was your last day on earth.

Wrap it all up with a single hook that tells the reader the big benefit for them inside the pages of your book and you're already better positioned to have a top-selling book than most self-published authors hitting the nonfiction category of Amazon right now.

Thinking about what makes you unique also leads beautifully into the next topic we need to cover: who do you think you are to write a book?

WRITING A MEMOIR—YOU STILL NEED A HOOK

Memoirs can be a great way to share experiences, help others see they aren't alone in their struggle, and pass on stories from generation to generation, but I have to tell you something important: memoirs are very challenging to market.

This is not to discourage you from writing a memoir. It's tremendously valuable to share your story. There will be someone who NEEDS your message, and your book could help them in a big way. Memoirs by celebrities and recognized leaders sell well, but if you're not a household name, you have a lot more work to do to get your story sold.

You might be tempted to just sit down and write your story for you. This is fine if you don't intend to sell the book.

If you want book sales, you need to write your book with the reader in mind. **That means you still need a hook.**

Many memoirs will share stories that help the reader to gain tools to overcome obstacles, experience emotions to gain confidence or clarity, or be encouraged to take action and face their situation head on. Ron Worley's book, *Ditches to Riches*, is a good example because it not only shares his story of hitting rock bottom but it also shares the Worley Way in order to help readers get out of their own ditches.

Your story can be incredibly powerful for others to learn, but for it to be highly marketable, you need to think carefully about what the reader will gain from reading it. And make sure it has a clear and specific outcome for that reader when they are done. Your marketing success depends on it.

CHAPTER 3:

YOUR SPECIAL GIFT

Your book could change someone's life. But are you the best person to write it?

To answer that question, you need to get clear on what makes you unique and *what you have to offer that is of unique value to others.*

We started this work to uncover the hook of your book. Now we're going to build on it. This will also lead beautifully into creating the outline for your book. Before we do that, pull out a pen and pad of paper. Write down these questions and start brainstorming to answer each one.

1. What outcome can you offer someone who reads your book?

2. What stories do you think you need to tell?

3. What common beliefs in your industry do you *not* believe?

4. What was one of your lowest moments or what was your biggest obstacle to achieving success in your work or personal life?

5. What has allowed you to succeed where others failed?

These important questions will help you define who you are and why you are the person to write your book. Defining yourself is essential to becoming the expert who stands out from the crowd and becomes well-known in your industry.

WHAT BRIAN GRAZER, ZZ TOP, LADY GAGA & BILL NYE THE SCIENCE GUY CAN TEACH YOU

Some of the most important lessons on becoming a successful author and building a great brand come from Hollywood.

Take this one, as an example. Brian Grazer is Hollywood elite. As of the start of 2018, his work had 131 Emmy Award nominations and 43 Academy Award nominations. He and his business partner Ron Howard have been behind some huge movies like *Splash, Backdraft,* and *Apollo 13,* to name some of their early successes. His company was also behind *Felicity, Arrested Development, 24,* and many other hit TV shows.[8]

Brian's work speaks for itself, doesn't it?

Not entirely.

In the mid-90s, as his star was starting to rise, he realized something important:

He needed something that differentiated him as a producer.

In an interview with author and investor Tim Ferriss,[9] he said, "Other successful producers had beards and facial hair…and they became known and recognizable because of that. I needed something of my own."

---

8   Jane Wallace, "Brian Grazer, Academy Award-Winning Producer," The Yale Center for Dyslexia & Creativity, accessed September 8, 2020, https://dyslexia.yale.edu/story/brian-grazer/.

9   Tim Ferriss, "Brian Grazer Interview: The Time Ferriss Show (Podcast)," YouTube, December 11, 2017, https://youtu.be/3-wA15Zt-6U.

Swimming in his pool with his young daughter one day, he spiked his hair, and she loved it. He looked in the mirror and thought, "Yup, that's it."

His hair has been spiked ever since. It's something that sets him apart and makes him easily recognizable.

You don't need to spike your hair, but you do need to differentiate yourself. You need to be known for something special to establish your brand.

Think about it: ZZ Top would be just another band without the beards. Lady Gaga wouldn't make so many headlines without her outrageous outfits. William Nye was just another scientist, until he labeled himself "Bill Nye the Science Guy."

In a media interview, I was referred to as Julie "The Book" Broad. It was so fun, I decided to use it on the introduction to all of my BookLaunchers.tv YouTube videos.

How do you want to be known in your marketplace?

BE COMES FIRST

If you're thinking you have to do X before you write your book, let me share something that has changed my approach in life and business: "Be, Do, Have."

This motto originated with the author and motivational speaker Zig Ziglar[10] but I learned it from renowned business entrepreneur Keith Cunningham.[11]

---

10 Ziglar Inc., "Be, Do and Have More – Zig Ziglar," YouTube, January 5, 2012, https://www.youtube.com/watch?v=QlWMZylMt5c.

11 If you're reading foot notes, yes, Keith Cunningham is the one I mentioned before as the source of so much of "Rich Dad" teachings. My parents signed me up for his Business Mentorship course in 2009 after I'd done the horrific act of quitting a six-figure job in the middle of a real estate crisis to grow two businesses in real estate. His mentorship was instrumental in helping me survive that financial crisis!

Be. Do. Have. That's the opposite of how most of us approach life. Most of us pursue our goals with the idea that *if we have X, we will do Y and be Z*. For example, I thought: when I **have** an MBA, I can do a job where I make six figures, and then I will **be** successful, have freedom, and feel financially secure.

It doesn't work that way. In fact, that line of thinking often takes you in the entirely *wrong* direction.

So many people think they first need to have the perfect story (achieve their pinnacle of success or some other huge milestone) to write a book and become the known expert.

You need to have material for your book, sure. But if you're waiting to have something before you do something so you can be someone, it's never going to happen.

The solution?

Figure out *who you want* to **be** first.

The way Keith explained it to me was: "*Who you be dictates what you do, and what you do dictates what you'll* **have**."

That's close to what I believe. Actually, I think it's about connecting to who you actually **are** and letting yourself **be** that person. That will dictate what you **do** and what you **have**.

Most of us resist who we really are.

We worry we won't be liked. For some of us, high school taught us to hide our opinions, dress like the most popular individuals, and not appear like we're trying too hard.

With lessons like those that hit so hard so early in life, it's no wonder we tend to hide our true selves, and the thought of showing people who we really are when we write a book is terrifying. But it holds us back. The fact is, if you try to hide who you really are and what you think, you're going to write a boring book. **The very thing that is going to make your book stand out and be amazing is YOU.**

Aspiring authors have all kinds of fear-based excuses: "I can't say the wrong thing or I'll be ostracized in my industry," "I have a successful business right now. I can't write anything to jeopardize it," and my favorite, "I just need to wait until I have achieved something great so it has the perfect ending."

It's very likely that you have a story inside you, but YOU need to believe it before anyone else can.[12]

At a FinCon conference for financial bloggers and podcasters, I met a lovely man who had more than a decade of experience in his area of expertise. He had a concept that would help others in his field, and there was only one other author in the marketplace at the time. An opportunity existed and he could see it. But he was stuck in his head. He said all kinds of things like, "Well, I'm not first. That other author probably has the market cornered."

The reality was that he was letting his ego run the show. When the ego runs the show, the monsters we all have in our closet come out in bold colors and loud noises. My biggest and noisiest monsters are fear of judgment and fear of failure. I think he was afraid of judgment, failure, and success, and those fears were all fighting for first place.

When I saw him two years later, he reported sadly that there were now nearly a dozen books covering his topic and, clearly, there was no longer any need for his book. Two of the new authors in the space had also started big live events, and one had a super successful podcast. He could have been one of the leaders in the space but he let fear control him.

---

12 Tim Testa, our Story Expert at Book Launchers, actually added this line to the manuscript. It's brilliant. Thanks Tim.

SOMEONE IS GOING TO BECOME FAMOUS DOING WHAT YOU DO. WHY NOT YOU?

If you're in the minority of people who think they don't have enough material for a book, think again. Have you ever heard of a self-help author named Napoleon Hill? His book, *Think and Grow Rich*, which was published in 1937, sold more than a hundred million copies worldwide. It's based on research, not his personal experience.

He studied individuals who built personal fortunes and shared what he learned. By doing the research, he became an expert.

Or have you heard of *Chicken Soup for the Soul?* That entire book series was born from Mark Victor Hansen and Jack Canfield's belief that inspirational stories had value.[13] They collected 101 stories to inspire, and voilà, an entire series—not to mention a consumer goods and media company—was born!

Still not convinced? Well, the *Wealthy Barber* by David Chilton and *Rich Dad Poor Dad* use fictional characters to teach important points around finance.[14]

If you have a message to share or something you believe in, and you feel compelled to get it out there, there's a way to do it with what you know and what you've accomplished to date. And if you know it will serve as the foundation for a business on the other side, what are you waiting for?

A successful book quickly adds a zero to most contracts, services, and speaking fees, making them far more lucrative and boosting your income!

Maybe you're thinking, "I'm too busy, I don't have time!" We're all busy.

---

13 "History," *Chicken Soup for the Soul*, accessed September 8, 2020, https://www.chickensoup.com/about/history.

14 Carrick, Rob. *The Wealthy Barber Returns*, The Globe and Mail, September 9, 2011, https://www.theglobeandmail.com/globe-investor/investment-ideas/the-wealthy-barber-returns/article1362752/.

I'll come back to this later in this book, but the more important question to ask yourself is:

Are you really too busy to find five hours a week to write (or work with a writer and a team) and get your book done, or is it just an excuse because you're afraid of what can happen if you commit to it?

Most people can clear 30 minutes a day to write. Maybe you can find time on your commute or at the doctor's office, maybe speaking into a recorder or making notes on your phone. Then, find an extra two hours on the weekend, maybe skipping some Netflix time, or getting up early instead of sleeping in on Sunday.

Plus, if you already create content for your work (videos, podcasts, blog posts, and newsletters), you probably have at least half a book already written! Once you have the hook for your book, you'll be able to develop an outline (keep reading…we're getting there). With that outline, you can see where you can take your existing content and drop it in.

The mistake many people make is starting with the content and trying to turn it into a book. That's backwards. Start with the hook, develop the concept, build the outline, and then drop in the content you already have and fill in the gaps!

FEW PEOPLE WILL MAKE A STRONG IMPACT WITHOUT AN EFFORT.

Maybe you just think you're not a good enough writer. Well, that's what editors are for, and if you do a lot of research and begin with a great outline, your book will almost write itself. If you hate writing and have a great outline, why don't you try recording it? You can talk like you were telling your friend the substance of your book and then have that transcribed. A great editor can work magic on those words and turn it into a book.

The upshot is, the reasons you think you can't write your book are just excuses. All you need is someone to kick your ass and get it done. Or you can hire Book Launchers because we've got a fantastic team of publishing professionals to help you out, including a writing coach who will work with you to craft a great outline and position your book so it appeals to your ideal reader and sells many copies. But keep reading because I am going to help you with a lot of that right now.

You may think everything that needs to be written about your topic has been written but there's always room for another approach. **Someone's going to become famous and help a lot of people doing what you do, so why not make it you?**

Most celebrities have worked hard to create strong brands. Oprah, Taylor Swift, Katy Perry, the Kardashians, and Adam Levine all have strong brands but not by accident.

Get to know your ideal reader. Get clear on the hook of your book. And differentiate yourself. One day soon, someone could say your book changed their life.

CHAPTER 4:

YOUR NOT-DO LIST

More things will go wrong when you write and publish a book than will go right.

Yes, this is the motivational section of my book.

Be prepared. It's not easy but it's worth it.

YOUR BOOK IS NOT A BUSINESS CARD

A good book is a thousand times better than a business card if you do it right. However, if you think of your book as just a "business card" book, it will probably end up being crap and then what's the point? The world doesn't need more garbage.

I have strong opinions on this, but I believe a book is valuable if it focuses on ways to have a big impact on its readers. **When you focus on your readers and what you need to do to create a great book for them, you're more likely to pursue excellence.** (Notice I said excellence, not perfection.)

Thinking of your book as something as disposable as a business card does not create excellence.

A business card book is something anyone can write. If you are serious about writing a book and furthering your career, you can't afford to be just anyone.

AVOID BREAKEVEN MENTALITY

Prospective authors often believe their book won't make money. I often hear them say, "I just want to break even." My question back is:

Why are you doing anything to just break even?

While many self-published books don't sell thousands of copies, those authors also didn't have a plan to generate income from their book. Book sales are not the only way a book generates an income, and when you stop looking just for breakeven, you can see huge potential.

Most authors write a book and then figure out how to market it. They hope it will grow their business or lead to speaking engagements. What I'm here to tell you is the opposite. Start with your goals, envision how you'll sell books and make money around the book, and build the book that can do that.

It still doesn't guarantee success because you have to execute on that plan and keep trying things to reach your readers, but it puts the odds on your side.

It's a lot of work to go through life just working to break even. How you define success matters. If you want to create a high-quality book, one that could sit on the shelves of Barnes & Noble or Chapters Indigo in Canada, then you're looking at investing somewhere between $6,000–$12,000 just for editing, layout, cover design, and a few other essential elements. That's not including a writer to help if you need it, nor does it factor anything in for marketing.

You'll have to sell between 1,000 and 2,000 copies to break even—maybe more, depending on your price point.

That might sound like a lot. But with the right plan, a great hook, and some daily effort, it's possible to sell 1,000 copies and, hopefully, a lot more!

Plus, I highly recommend you use your book as a tool to generate multiple streams of income so you aren't relying on book sales alone. (More on that in a moment.)

WHAT IS YOUR GOAL FOR YOUR BOOK?

While I want you to focus on your ideal reader when you write your book, you should have a big picture vision of how you'll use your book as a tool in your career or business. Being clear on your goal for a reader ensures that you write a book with impact, and it also helps you keep your imposter syndrome and fear monsters in the closet. Knowing your reader's goal, however, isn't enough to direct the content of your book to be exactly what you need for yourself.

Are you writing a book to get new clients, raise your prices, or land paid speaking gigs? Will media interviews help your business? Possibly, you want to sell online courses or fill live events? Maybe you're hoping to secure a TV or a movie deal?

Ryan Berman wrote *Return on Courage* to support his new career as a paid speaker. While writing the book, he included stories of courage from major corporations like Google and Snapchat in part because he loved the stories but also in the hopes that they would be more likely to have him speak at their organizations. This was a smart way to get him engagements with those companies. With big brand experience behind him, he could then leverage his expertise, along with the book content, for paid speaking gigs with even more businesses. A video of Ryan telling that story is at booklaunchers.com/notboring

Sure, maybe your book only sells 500 copies but if those copies lead to new clients, higher rates, or paid speaking gigs, your book more than pays for itself!

It's nice to write a best-selling book but having that as a primary goal means you are being driven more by ego than results. It's much more important to make sure your book achieves your business goal.

OVERALL BOOK GOAL	CORE STRATEGY	SUPPLEMENTAL STRATEGY
MAKE MONEY FROM BOOK SALES	*Write to market and set up your accounts for maximum payout*	*Build a strong platform while you write multiple books to create a series, repackage series as a box set*
BECOME A PAID PROFESSIONAL SPEAKER	*Strategic relationships to get your book in front of the people who book paid speakers*	*Utilize the book to get PR – TV, Radio, Print, and Podcast media will all build credibility that will boost your position as an expert to be paid to speak*
ATTRACT NEW CLIENTS	*Strategic relationships to get your book in front of people who have groups of your ideal readers already in their audience*	*A strong push for Amazon reviews and sales to build your book's reputation to attract other book promotional opportunities and get it in front of more of your ideal readers*
RAISE YOUR PROFILE/ BECOME THE KNOWN EXPERT IN YOUR NICHE	*Strategic relationships to get your book in front of the people who will introduce you to people in their audience*	*Utilize the book to get PR*
SELL PRODUCTS, COURSES, OR SERVICES	*Market to your existing network and community*	*A strong push for Amazon reviews and sales to build your book's reputation to attract other book promotional opportunities and get it in front of more of your ideal readers*

Ways to 10X Your Book Investment.

Of course, it depends on your goals and your business, but the right book positioned well can easily lead to big returns, including:

- Paid speaking gigs
- New clients
- The ability to charge more for your services
- A strategic partnership
- Media exposure
- Financial opportunities, such as capital for your business (if you're a real estate investor, this could be a game changer!)
- Brand extensions, including swag, courses, or workshops
- The sale of your business

The person who is known as *The Person* to hire for something can charge far more for exactly the same service as someone who isn't well-known. Imagine if you hired a home organizer to clean out your clutter. You're probably going to pay $25–$40 per hour for their services, right? Now imagine if celebrity Marie Kondo herself was coming to your house. You're probably going to pay thousands of dollars for the same service but she's Marie Kondo, "The Organizing Person."

You probably already knew a book would position you as an expert to get paid to speak. I'm sure you know that the right book can also attract new clients and even help raise your rates. Books are also powerful business boosters *even if you're selling a product!*

If you were one of the most well-known names in your niche, how much could you charge?

Consider what Dave Asprey, author of five books and founder and CEO of Bulletproof Coffee, told digital marketers at the Traffic & Conversion Summit in 2018:

"People who have read one of my books buy twice as much from us as the people who haven't read one of my books."

The right book is going to elevate your business, increase your profile, and likely boost your income, whether you're providing a service or selling a product.

Take a moment right now and start brainstorming all the ways you could multiply your investment by writing a book.

GREAT BOOK + BAD TITLE = NO BOOK SALES

"This might sound like I'm critical of avid book readers…and I'm not. But those people will read almost anything. The trick is getting it in front of them."

A public relations professional said that to me during a recent chat. She's behind some pretty incredible success stories, including a *New York Times* best-selling author who is now a paid professional speaker booked 172 days a year. His book even became a movie. After working as a talent agent, a PR pro, and a talent manager, she had a lot of insights.

One of the things we spoke about was this:

The best marketing plan in the world won't help you if you have a terrible book title.

When Michael Brenner brought us his book, for example, he called it *The Empathy Formula*. Do you want to read that or do you want to read *Mean People Suck*?

The title is what people will have to remember to find your book. It's what people will share when they tell others about it. And, ultimately, it's what gets a reader's attention (or doesn't).

In another instance, an author contacted me looking for help marketing his book about male infertility. He worked with a company that helped him write the book, edit it, and get it on Amazon. He figured once it was on Amazon, with the right tags and a good book description, it would sell itself.

After six months, he had sold 20 copies. I saw his book was well-written, personal, and engaging. It had a clear hook and a defined audience. The problem was not the content. The issue was that he had the same title as eight other books. The title didn't sell the book, the subtitle didn't have any keywords, and the cover wasn't good enough to help either.

I explained that to him and discussed how we could fix those issues.

"I'd rather you try to market it the way it is now," he replied. "And if it still doesn't sell, I'll consider making the changes."

I suggested he work with someone else.

I'm in the business of creating success stories, and even the best marketing plan in the world would have trouble overcoming the hurdles he'd created.

I'll cover the other challenges with his book soon but for now let's talk about titles. Yes, **two different books can have the same title.** For the most part, titles can't be copyrighted. That means you can use the same title. The bigger question is, do you want to? (Watch the video at booklaunchers.com/notboring for more details.)

At Book Launchers, we take titles and subtitles very seriously and spend dozens of hours brainstorming and developing book titles and subtitles, chapter titles, and book positioning statements for our clients. We look at the category, competitive and keyword research, and try to craft a compelling title for readers and search engines. Book descriptions and author bios are also written with keyword research in mind.

We have a Slack channel dedicated to titles and subtitles and another one for Table of Contents brainstorming. It's expected that everyone in the company contribute to brainstorming, from the person who builds our websites to the person in charge of operations. Often, it's the off the wall idea that inspires the winning idea so everyone's input is needed. That's also how important it is to help our clients stand out.

One of our clients was skeptical about our recommended title. Smartly, he tested the waters in a big Facebook group to which he belongs.

"These people are all writers in my industry, so they're used to writing catchy titles and subtitles," he told us. "Clearly, you and your team know what you're doing because your suggestion was the hands-down winner. Nothing else was even close."

A great book title will be unique, capture attention, create curiosity, and be easy to remember. So does your title check off all the boxes? Let's make sure.

#1 Is it short? Three words or less is ideal.

This is a guideline not a rule, and as soon as I tell you this you're going to point to the exceptions to this rule, of course—exceptions like *How to Win Friends and Influence People, The Subtle Art of Not Giving a F*ck , and The 7 Habits of Highly Effective People.* However, the majority of best-selling books in nonfiction categories, and even in fiction, tend to be three words or less.

Check out the top 20 best-selling business books for the year, and I bet 75 percent or more have short titles like these:

- *Lean In*
- *Outliers*
- *Becoming*
- *Start with Why*
- *Good to Great*
- *Open Book*
- *Educated*

You get the point. You might have a title that could be an exception, but it's generally a good idea to stick with a punchy, to-the-point title, and sell your reader in the subtitle.

#2 Is it easy to remember?

This is the test I should have done for my second book, *The New Brand You*, so learn from my mistake.

Tell your friends what you're thinking of calling your book. A few hours later say, "Hey listen, do you remember my book title?"

Don't tell them that this is a test because then they'll make sure to remember. You want to find out if your book title is memorable. You want people to be able to spread the word and remember the title themselves when they go to buy the book. If I had done this, I would have discovered that nobody could remember it! It always came out in some twisted, not-quite-right version—usually, *The Brand New You*.

#3 Is it easy to say?

Now you might be thinking, "Why does that matter for something people are reading?"

If you're doing a great job of selling your book, you're going to be talking about your book all the time. And other people will be saying the title all the time. There's nothing more embarrassing than doing a media interview when the host can't remember your correct book title. Again, learn from my mistake! There are dozens of podcast interviews out there with the host getting my title wrong.

Say your title over and over and over again. Do you still like it? Ask a few friends to do the same thing. Do they find that it is still easy to say after repeating it several times? Great, check it off.

#4 Is it taken? (Bonus points if the URL for your book title is available.)

You're probably writing your book to position yourself as the authority in your marketplace, right? Now imagine a potential reader types your book title into Google and finds four other books and a website and none are yours. **That makes it difficult to position yourself as the leader in this category.**

If you're considering a series of books, a workshop, products, or an app to monetize your book in other ways, owning your book's URL makes all of that much easier.

While you're searching for the URL, it's also a good time to gut check what else you come across. S.A. Bradley's book *Screaming for Pleasure* is a great title in the horror genre but when it first came out, you had to know what it was about to find it. Now that it's been out for a long time, the search results are dominated by his book links, but that wasn't always the case. And, let me tell you, the other results had nothing to do with horror.

#5 Does your title pop?

A great book on this subject is *Pop!* by Sam Horn. She talks about how to break out from the pack. By that, she means you want to make sure that your book title stands out and doesn't sound like every other book in its category. Think about what will create curiosity. What will have people grab your book, excited to read it?

Ask yourself: Can you check off all five of these criteria? Even if you can, you should run a few tests just to be sure that your title will have people running to the store to buy your book. It's rare an author comes to Book Launchers with a title that is anywhere near as good as they think it is. It's more common to find an author has fallen in love with a title that runs counter to most of these points.

How do you do that? If you have an email newsletter, you can send out a survey with two or more choices. Ask people to select their preference ("Would you want to buy this book or this book?"). See which one is more popular and is most likely to get people buying your book.

The subtitle is an entirely different matter. As noted above, we use keywords in brainstorming subtitles, and we apply principles of copywriting to the creation of a great subtitle. Remember, the role of the title is to get attention and be easy to sell. The role of the subtitle is to actually sell your book to the ideal reader AND to the search engines.

In many ways, the subtitle is a summary of your hook. Here's a few examples of Book Launchers author's book subtitles we love:

1. *Protecting the Pig: How Stock Market Trends Reveal the Way to Grow and Preserve Your Wealth*

The subtitle makes it really clear what the book is about and what you'll gain from reading the book. You'll read that and know it's the book for you (or not). It's also keyword rich.

2. *Tactical Lock Picking: A Systemized Approach for Responding to Locked Obstacles During Emergencies*

This is also such a strong title and subtitle combination because it's very clear who is going to want to read the book and why they would want to read it. The title and subtitle have some keywords in them. Not surprisingly, the book has been very popular amongst the emergency responder audiences.

Ultimately, it's a great subtitle if you can understand who it's for, what the book is about, and what you'll gain after you've read it.

FAKE NAMES = FAKE FEELS AROUND MARKETING

Michael Masterson, a best-selling author and entrepreneur, was my virtual mentor before I started my first online business. I read every one of his daily e-newsletters and read all his books. When he had a conference in Florida, I took time off from my job and spent thousands of dollars to be there.

When I eventually met him, I found out his real name wasn't Michael Masterson. It was Mark Ford.

Clients knew him as Michael. Colleagues knew him as Mark. His team called him Mark, but when in the presence of clients they had to remember to call him Michael. They often stumbled on this.

Over time, I developed a relationship with the company and had the honor of writing articles for their newsletter. I even became a promotional partner with my first online course. But I was still in this weird spot, what do I call him? I didn't know whether to call him Michael or Mark.

I never asked him directly why he used a pen name, but I did Google him to try to figure it out. I wondered if he was hiding something. I eventually found out his penname was an editorial choice by the publishing company he was working with to build Early to Rise. They were building products under his pen name because they wanted it to be something they could use after he retired.[15]

I'll always be grateful for the start he and his company gave me in the online business world, but the fact that he had a pen name was uncomfortable and weird at the time.

With that in mind, let's talk about whether it makes sense for you.

GOOD REASONS TO USE A PEN NAME

Perhaps, you have a famous parent, or you're known for something else, and you want to chart your own course without the burden or benefit of that name. Those are great reasons to use a pen name but such situations are not common.

---

15 Mark Morgan Ford, "Dos and Donts [sic] with Pen Names," Early to Rise, March 25, 2008, https://www.earlytorise.com/dos-and-donts-with-pen-names/.

In some cases, you may want to build brands around two totally different subjects and use a pen name to avoid confusion between the two. If you write fiction and nonfiction, a pen name could make a lot of sense. I'd recommend using a pen name for fiction and your real name for nonfiction.

If you're a whistleblower and need to maintain confidentiality for reasons of security or employment, you'll face some credibility challenges but your decision to use a pen name is understandable.

Possibly, you want a cooler or more marketable name if your real name is long or particularly difficult to pronounce. We're not all born Broads (which is pronounced Broad—as in wide, not Brode, like The Broad Museum in LA. I mean, my family is great, but we're not those Broads).

MOST NONFICTION AUTHORS SHOULD NOT USE A PEN NAME. HERE'S WHY.

You are most likely writing this book to grow your business and build your brand. That's very difficult to do if people find out it's not actually you. You risk losing trust and credibility when you use a pen name. Stick with your own name to establish trust, build credibility, and show who you are and what you know.

When somebody knows you under your pen name and also knows you personally with your real name, how do they introduce you? When you go to a conference, what do you put on your name tag? Like I said, I didn't know whether to call Mark, Michael, or Michael, Mark. It made me quite uncomfortable.

Finally, using your own name makes it easier to market your work. Even if you're writing in different categories, cross-promotion can be helpful, and some people will read everything you write, regardless of genre.

A pen name also complicates your author platform and social media. Do you put a fake picture, a blacked-out image, or just an impersonal logo on your page? Even though social media doesn't typically directly sell a lot of books, it does have value for authors.

More things may go wrong than right while writing a book. Now that you know what those things are, a lot may still go wrong but it won't cause you to fail.

CHAPTER 5:

HOW TO SAVE 1,418 HOURS WRITING YOUR NEXT BOOK

You're busy. You don't have time to waste. In other words, you need this chapter.

First, I have a confession. I don't have a proprietary method of book writing that will save you 1,418 hours. I made up that number so you'd be intrigued. (When it comes to your book, every chapter title needs to be so interesting it could sell your book on its own and even attract speaking gigs and media invites.)

Here's the good news, though: you can probably write the first draft of your book in fewer than 100 hours.

You may have just collapsed on the floor, screaming, "One hundred hours?"

That's only two and a half weeks if you work on it full time. Really, that's not a bad time investment for something that can easily make you six figures or more if you do it right!

That's 20 weeks or 4.5 months if you write 5 hours a week.

You can even write your book in under 40 hours if you have help! Our ghostwriters can spend fewer than 40 hours with you and get you to a completed first draft.

But I have to warn you that it could take even longer than 100 hours if you don't have a plan. Even if you hire a great writer to help you, without a great plan, your book will take a long time to write.

I WRITE BETTER WITHOUT AN OUTLINE, OR SO I THOUGHT

I'd hate to guess how many hundreds of hours I spent writing my first two books. I didn't have help or a plan for either one.

The most painful thing is that I not only wasted a lot of time struggling to write my books but also that I wrote a ton of material that didn't make it into the final manuscripts.

Sure, that content doesn't have to be wasted. You can post it on your website, use it in newsletters, or turn it into course material. While that is all true, my process was still totally inefficient and more costly than it needed to be. Editors charge on a per-word basis, so editing cost me a lot more for an 80,000-word manuscript than it would have for the 65,000 words that remained when she was done. The time that went into those cut 15,000 words is time I won't get back either. And I should tell you, it wasn't just cutting out 15,000 words. We actually cut more than that and I had to spend time writing the other material that the editor felt was missing!

Everyone has limited time so being efficient should be your highest priority. Money can be earned again but time is gone forever. Spend a dozen hours before you write to save you 100 hours later.

Once you are clear on your audience, you have crafted the hook of your book and you know how you'll differentiate yourself, it's time to build your book outline. This is going to be your roadmap to get you to the first draft.

BUILD YOUR BOOK BACKWARDS

The vast majority of nonfiction authors write using an outline. Yes, there are exceptions, but when you ask non-outliners about their process, they will tell you they often write themselves into a corner and have to do some massive rewrites to get out. (Hi! That was me for my first two books.)

Your other writing experiences may give you the impression that you don't need an outline but don't fall for it.

Nothing in real life plays out the way you think it will. Few people really plan for catastrophes. Earthquake—sure. Global pandemic—nope. Figuring out how to work at home with no support and children unable to go to school is a scenario that hit working families all over the world with Covid-19.

The unexpected happens. That's real life.

But rarely does anyone anticipate their spouse getting cancer or having a job suddenly transfer you across the country. Freak accidents, tragedies, and happy surprises happen to everyone.

You might wonder, then what is the point of planning?

When it comes to writing a book, this is the point: When the unexpected sidelines your book, as it undoubtedly will, you have a plan and can pick up where you left off. And that will save you tons of time.

The only problem is that you won't be able to hammer out a brilliant outline in a day. It can be tricky to know what's important to include in a book and what needs to be cut! Then there's also that pesky personal doubt that will creep in as you try to figure out what killer tips you'll share.

An outline isn't as simple as you might hope. Plus, you need to know whether each section fits with your hook or not, which takes time too.

Emotional and time challenges aside, there are three main approaches to outlines. Personally, I'm all about bullet points. I write a list of my topics, put bullet points under them covering my key points, and then see what's missing or whether it's in the right order. But for others, like Ryan Holiday, author of *Perennial Seller,* using notecards is the best method. (He wrote about this on Medium. You can find a link to the article at booklaunchers.com/notboring)

Mindmaps work for other authors.

No one method works for everyone so check out these three strategies and/or find one that will work for you. Alternatively, know that you can get help with outlines. Some of our clients will never create an outline. Instead, working with our Story Expert or a Writing Coach, the client does a brain dump of all their topics and our team member organizes them into a professional outline. Some brains are just better suited to organizing the data than others. Know your strengths and get help with the rest—a book is a gigantic project and you will need help.

NOTE CARD OUTLINING

The benefit of this approach is that you can physically reorganize your thoughts. To keep the process more organized, buy a package of tri-colored 3×5 index cards. Assign colors for each of the three parts of a chapter:

1. **Chapter Subject:** the main point of the chapter

2. **Chapter Topics:** 3–5 topics that expand on the chapter subject

3. **Chapter Subtopics:** 3–5 subtopics that expand on the chapter topics

Take 12–15 note cards of one color and write down an idea for a chapter on each card. For instance, if you're writing a book on running chapter subjects might include:

- Equipment
- Nutrition
- Myths
- Injury Prevention
- Training Schedules

Each subject gets its own card. *Your introduction doesn't count, so if one of your cards is your intro, add another one for a chapter heading.*

Once you have 12–15 note cards, assess them. Do all of these subjects really need their own chapter? Can some of them be combined into one? If they can, staple those cards together.

Do any of the cards not really belong? Toss them! Having a fat book is not as important as having satisfied readers. Keep your book fluff-free! There are almost always a couple of subjects you think should be in your book, but when you lay out all the topics, you can see that some of them just aren't meaty enough to be their own chapter.

Determining the size of a chapter, and ultimately your book size also can be a challenge, and every chapter will not be the same length. Let me first say there is no rule about how long your book must be. Nor is there a rule that a chapter should not contain more than X number of words.

For overall book size, we generally encourage our clients to shoot for at least 35,000 words so the book can be at least 110 pages long without excessive spacing to fill in the pages. This allows the book to be thick enough to put the title on the spine and feel more like a book than a brochure.

The typical book we help publish is about 50,000–60,000 words. Published into a print book that ends up being 180–240 pages. These books typically have 12–24 chapters, but again, there are always exceptions. A random survey of *New York Times* Best-Selling Business Books in 2020 shows they have a median average length of 347 pages with 18 chapters.

There is no right length for your book. Let your subject be your guide.

You also have to take into account if you're going to have diagrams, pictures, illustrations, addendums, and other things though. All of those kinds of things will add pages to your book as well.

As an estimate, if you're trying to figure out the length of your manuscript, a page in a standard 6" x 9" book contains about 250 words per page.

Now once you have a sense of the overall size, you can think about chapters. Obviously, if your book is a total of 35,000 words, it does not make sense to have a 10,000-word chapter. Your chapters should be less than 5,000 words, with some shorter and some longer. If you're writing a longer book, you may have a few chapters exceeding 5,000 words.

Personally, I think you want a minimum of eight chapters for this length book but there are no rules. This is your book. Look at your competition to get a feel for it. What is common in your genre? What seems right when you read your book?

Most important, ***make sure that your chapters align with the hook of your book***. In the middle of your brilliant "How to Invest Wisely in a Down Economy," for example, don't squeeze in a chapter about your dancing prowess and how many people know you as Vinny, the dancing machine.

Write out 3–5 cards for topics within chapters and explain them. To go back to our 5K running example, you might add Stretching, Hydration, Gradual Increases in Speed, and Slow Increases in Distances to a chapter on Injury Prevention.

Finally, add your remaining color-coded cards. On these cards, write detailed subtopics for each topic. For example, under Stretching, you could discuss yoga moves, when to stretch, how long to stretch, and the best stretches for dealing with shin splints.

The big benefit of this method is being able to manually move pieces around, see what topics don't have enough cards, and reorganize quickly. However, be aware that you may lose a card!

Keep them carefully organized in one place. You can use a recipe card box to store them and, once you have them in order, put a number in the bottom corner of each card.

MIND MAPPING A BOOK OUTLINE

If you prefer to work visually and more creatively, this might be for you, especially if you like online software options like Bubl.us or mindmeister.com. Just make sure you print and save your mind map and know how to access it later.

How it works:

To mind map, start with your working title in the center.

As you think of chapter headings, create circles that connect to the center. As details and topics occur to you, place them in headings or subheadings under that topic.

Populate your map over several days, letting your mind explore all the possibilities.

Play with the map and see how many circles you can derive from the center.

As you fill in circles on your map, notice if it gets to be lopsided. Does a chapter subject not have enough topics to support it? You may need to reorganize or combine some topics. Does one chapter have a bunch of topics? Maybe it should be split into two.

The Mind Map is really helpful for authors who have lots of ideas but don't necessarily come up with their ideas in any discernible order. It's a great way to get all your thoughts onto paper and then explore the topics you want to cover. A mind map can become a distraction, however, if you lose focus easily. It can also be overwhelming if you are someone who likes order.

BULLET POINT LISTS

No matter what advancements in technology emerge to help people with time management and productivity, I am a list maker on paper. I write lists for everything. Buying groceries, managing my team, getting my work done, and packing for trips. I wouldn't manage any of these things without handwritten lists.

If you make to-do lists and automatically group items according to where or when you plan on executing them, this is probably the right method to outline your book.

If you have a good sense of steps 1, 2, and 3 in your book, start here. **How it works:**

- Make a list of 10–12 high level bullet points that you want to discuss in your book.
- Create 3–5 sub points for each subject.
- Write 3–5 words that will help you remember what each sub point means.
- Evaluate the subjects and topics. Cut or reorganize bullet points that are duplicated, don't have enough sub points or don't make sense in the context of the entire book.
- Reorganize the bullet points in an order that makes sense to you.

Example:

- 5K Book
  - Equipment
    - Footwear
      - Importance of proper fitting
      - Pronate vs. Supinate
      - Arch support
    - Apparel
      - Breathability
      - Cotton Is Rotten
      - Chaffing
    - Safety Gear
      - Lights
      - Reflective Wear
  - Nutrition
    - What your body needs while you run
    - What your body needs after you run
    - What to eat while you are training
  - Training Programs
    - 12-week
    - 10-week
    - 8-week
  - Injury Prevention
    - Stretching
    - Slowly increase speed
    - Slowly increase distance

(Thanks to Jaqueline Kyle from our Book Launchers team for sketching this out for our clients and website—it fits perfectly into the book too. ☺)

This method also looks like a table of contents and allows you to see your book coming to life!

With this, you have an approach to create the outline and save dozens of hours writing your book. Before you dive in and start writing, have someone else look at your outline to see if it makes sense. Do they feel anything is missing or too heavily covered? It's your book but another perspective helps.

Move on to identify research, stories, quotes, and any other material you need to gather to write your book.

If you ever sit down and feel like you don't know what to write, it's probably because you didn't do the research or planning well enough for that section. Do the prep, so when you have 30 minutes, you can sit down and work on a section!

CREATING A KILLER TABLE OF CONTENTS

This step is not designed to pressure you to make this outline perfect right now but only to plant the seed that you need to develop every chapter title to be so strong it can sell your book on its own. For now, your goal is an outline that will help you create a bad first draft. **That's your first goal, by the way: A bad first draft.** Set your mind to anything greater than that and I'll have published two or three new editions of this book before you've even sent your book to an editor.

Far too many authors do not spend enough time on their table of contents. That's a problem because it not only needs to sell your book but it also can lead to speaking engagements and media interviews.

When I self-published my first two books, nobody told me this. In fact, despite spending nearly $8,000 on each book for editors and hiring professionals to make it as good as possible, not a single person spent any time on the table of contents except for the editor working on formatting and typos. That's a darn shame.

I look at my first two books and I see some decent chapter titles, but I also see some that could've been so much better if someone had just told me I should be working on them as hard as I worked on my book titles.

I'm doing that for you right now.

You can start writing without having the perfect book title or chapter title. But when you're done, these chapter titles need to be researched and tested to make each one as good as it possibly can be.

CHAPTER TITLES SELL BOOKS

If a reader likes your book cover and title and the reviews are decent, they're going to pick it up and flip to the inside in a bookstore or click on the *Look Inside* feature on Amazon. If that table of contents or those chapter titles aren't making them even more curious, you're probably going to lose them.

Most chapter titles sound like every other book in their genre.

I see the same one all the time: Finding Your Why. Seriously, all the time.

In real estate, I constantly see these chapter titles:

- Finding a Market to Invest In
- Calculating Your Cashflow
- Evaluating Investment Properties

Snooze. They're in every book already. It doesn't need to be in your book. If your reader has already consumed one self-help book or one real estate book and sees those chapter titles in yours, they'll feel like they don't need to read it.

"Finding Your Why" appeared as a chapter title in a self-help book published by one of our clients.

We suggested the author change it so that it:

- Promises to benefit the reader (ideally) in ways that can be quantified.
- Creates curiosity about something that's not already familiar to them.

- Generates controversy or contradicts commonly held beliefs.

We workshopped the title and came up with:

- Dreams and Escape Plans
- Dancing Around Your Dream
- There's a Difference Between a Dream and an Escape Plan
- Your Dreams in a Trust

These were all related to content in that chapter, but just as important, they were also far more interesting than "Finding Your Why."

The best chapter titles can stand alone as a title to a presentation, a course name, or a workshop offering. Of course, it has to be relevant and summarize your chapter, at least to a point. And, if it's in your book, it needs to fit your hook!

Try to hint at what you say in a chapter with a title that is a little different than the norm. Even if what you're covering doesn't vary much from industry practice—such as how to calculate your investment property cashflow—you can offer a title that makes it more specific or interesting. Teach someone how to "Calculate Cashflow without a Calculator" or introduce "The 5-Second Approach to Calculate Cashflow" or "The 3-Digit Formula for Cashflow Calculations."

Here's how to conduct a little test of your chapter titles. Show the table of contents to someone who hasn't read your book yet. See if they point to any chapters and say, "OOOH, I have to read this chapter!" When you get somebody saying that, you know you are on the right track for great chapter titles. Win!

QUICK SIDE NOTE ABOUT SOFTWARE

When I began writing one of my books, I bought Scrivener, a writing software that all my writer friends told me I had to use. They have a free trial period, but I just went ahead and bought it because I was so sure I would love it.

I excitedly opened it up on my computer and immediately thought, what the heck?

I saw a blank page and did what every writer probably does—I wrote the one thing I was sure I would put on paper: "Chapter 1."

Then I noticed a "corkboard" feature, so I ended up messing around with that. Then, I messed with organizing things by chapter. I took my outline and spent an hour setting up chapters. When that was done, I wanted to start writing, but I struggled to find a few things that are normal functions in Word so I watched YouTube videos to figure it out. That led me to all these other features.

Five hours into it, I hadn't written a word!

The secret to writing is to just sit your butt down and get to work.

Spend time writing a book that is interesting, engaging, and delivering a ton of value for your ideal reader. Don't waste time pursuing the best writing software.

Get the words on a page. You'll use other software to design your book for publication, so right now, your only real concern is getting the book out of your head. I'm especially talking to you if you're the kind of person who's going to research the heck out of this. What do you currently use to type up a document? That's the software you should use to write your book. Period. You know it, you're comfortable in it, your energy can go toward the most important thing you need to worry about, and that is making sure that you're writing— and that it's good.

TIME SPENT PLANNING IS TIME SAVED WRITING

Take time to outline your book because it will save you time. Figure out your hook because it will make your book marketable. And plan to write, publish, and market a book that will stand out because you're investing in creating the best possible product.

Just because it's easier than ever to self-publish doesn't mean you should if you're not prepared to create a great plan (your outline) and do it well.

If you take my advice, I may not have saved you 1,418 hours, but I guarantee I've saved enough of your valuable time to pay for this book and whatever you're drinking. Maybe even more.

CHAPTER 6:

THE SURPRISING SECRETS OF SPEED WRITING

You can write your book while you wait at the doctor's office, your car gets an oil change, or your kids are in swimming lessons.

You have a powerful piece of equipment in your hands right now. If your mobile device is not in your hand, I bet it's within arm's reach. Sure, your typing proficiency may not be 120 words per minute but you can jot down ideas, quotes, and even craft some stories while you're waiting. You can pull out the voice recording app and start talking. Guess what? You can also use a pen and paper.

The point is, you always have time to write as long as you're not looking for the perfect time or place to get it done.

Heck, romance novelist Amy Daws had writer's block until she took her car for new tires at a local South Dakota tire shop and discovered that was her Zen place for writing. She even began volunteering to take in the cars of family and friends, to the point that Tires Tires Tires gave her a reserved seat in their waiting room. When her book came out, they promoted it on their sign out front![16]

---

16 Amy Daws, "Tires Tires Tires," Love Stories by Amy Daws, accessed September 3, 2020, https://amydawsauthor.com/tirestirestires/.

If you're committed to getting your book done, you'll find the time to get it done. You just need a great plan (hint: an outline, see the previous chapter) so you can make use of your spare time.

PATIENCE IS PART OF THE PROMISED PATH

Writing is a lot like going to the gym. You know it's good for you and benefits are enormous but it can feel like a lot of effort just to get out the door.

You may enthusiastically start working out the first week or two but then you have a bad night of sleep or you're extra busy one week and the next thing you know, your couch is more appealing than the gym.

The same thing happens when you write a book. Many would-be authors report having an incredibly clean house as a result of their attempts to write a book. Others finally get their inbox to zero! Heck, you may find it's suddenly easier to get your taxes done early!

Things you normally avoid become important now that you have something bigger to avoid, and that's writing a book!

Steven Pressfield, in his brilliant book, *The War of Art*, defines obstacles between you and writing as the "Resistance." He says,

> *"Resistance is fear. But Resistance is too cunning to show itself naked in this form."* [17]

Your fear shows up in such rational ways that it's almost impossible to know that it's holding you back. For instance,

- One of your children gets in trouble at school.
- Work gets really busy or is unusually slow.

---

17 Steven Pressfield, *The War of Art* (New York: Black Irish Entertainment, 2002), 55.

- You find yourself getting sick or someone in your house is getting sick.
- Too many interesting opportunities to pass up.

You're probably reading that list thinking those are all totally legitimate reasons to not write a book. They provide you with great excuses not to write and that is exactly why the Resistance is so powerful.

We had a client dealing with his wife's cancer in the middle of writing his book. He almost gave up on it, but in his Unboxing video (booklaunchers.com/notboring) he compared our Story Expert, Tim Testa, to a "fireman carrying him over the finish line" so that he could get his book done.

There IS a way for you to write your book if you've decided to get it done.

Be patient. Determine that you're going to fight the Resistance every single day. Remind yourself that starting a book is exciting. Understand that finishing it is painful and takes discipline above all else.

Pressfield describes it this way:

> *"The professional steels himself at the start of a project, reminding himself it is the Iditarod, not the sixty-yard dash. He conserves his energy. He prepares his mind for the long haul."*[18]

To prepare you for the long haul, let's create a writing plan.

THE THREE Ts OF SPEEDY BOOK WRITING

Having a clear reason for your book and a plan (your outline) will help motivate you on those days when you just don't feel like it. And the Three Ts will help you write faster than ever before.

---

18   Pressfield, *The War of Art*, 76.

Topic for Tomorrow: When you finish writing for the day, note what you will start writing the next time you sit down. This is essential because you don't want to waste 30 minutes reading the stuff you wrote last time to refresh your memory and get warmed up.

Let me repeat that, with a slightly different emphasis: **when you sit down to write tomorrow, DO NOT READ what you wrote the day before.**

Every single time you finish writing and wrap up for the day, start your next section. Include some rough bullet points for what you're planning to cover. Then, when you sit down to write the next time, focus ONLY on those points.

Too many writers go back and read what they've written before, judge it, change it, and then before they've done any more writing, their time is over. It's even worse when you stare at a blank screen and wonder what you're going to write about.

Know before you sit down.

If you happen to get 20 minutes of free time, use that 20 minutes to write! If you do that five times a week following this plan, I bet you'll have your book done before you know it!

Target: Always have a goal. Perhaps, you'll sit and write for 30 minutes a day every weekday. That's how I work. I set a timer for a 45-minute writing session and turn everything else off. You could also decide to set a target of 500 or 2,000 words per day.

Ideally, you are accountable to someone so that you aren't the only one who knows about this target. We'll talk more about that in a second.

Time: Dedicate a specific time to writing your book. Figure out when you are the most productive and try to lock down that time a few days a week, or even every day.

I know you're thinking, "I have kids…I run a business…. There are always fires to put out."

Great ideas and powerful visions are worthless if you do nothing to bring them to life. For me, I have had to get up at 5:00 a.m. and write before my son gets up at 6:30 a.m. I don't enjoy waking up that early but I have things that are important to accomplish and that's how I get it done.

As coauthors, Brian Moran and Michael Lennington write in *The 12 Week Year*, "Execution is the single greatest market differentiator. Great companies and successful individuals execute better than their competition."[19]

Period. It's as simple, and as difficult, as making the time.

CHANGE ONE WORD TO CHANGE YOUR RESULTS

If I can show you a simple trick to help you finish your book, will you use it?

It all comes down to eliminating one three-letter word from your vocabulary:

Try.

You aren't TRYING to write a book. You ARE writing a book.

You aren't TRYING to build your business. You ARE building your business.

---

19   Brian P. Moran and Michael Lennington, *The 12 Week Year: Get More Done in 12 Weeks than Others Do in 12 Months* (New Jersey: Wiley, 2013).

Make your word your bond. Commit to it. Now.

If you allow yourself wiggle room for excuses in your language, your mind feels it, and you open yourself up to the possibility of massive failure. The word "try" is a crack in the foundation of your success. You start, you build, and you do the things you need to do to get to the result you want.

Or if you can recite the classic Yoda line:

"Do. Or do not. There is no try."[20]

When you stop trying and start doing, the results will astound you. Get to it.

THE ULTIMATE SPEED TIP FOR BOOK WRITING

If you've ever trained for a running race, you probably followed a training program with a mix of long runs, shorter faster runs, and sprints.

There were probably sprints combined with hill training too.

Training prepares you to be fitter and faster on race day, and it works. We apply these same principles during Book Launchers' writer's retreats and online writing sessions. Long stretches of writing are mixed with some short sprints.

The results have been incredible. One client, Leslie Quinsay, an expert investor and author, said, "I wrote more in two days than I have in months!" A big chunk of that success was due to the writing sprints. In 15 minutes, many of the authors reported writing up to 600 words! These sprints added up to big progress!

If you think you don't have time but you really want to write your own book, all you need is to carve out a spare 20 minutes a few times

---

20   https://www.youtube.com/watch?v=h5SNAluOj6U

a week. Within a month, you'll have at least one quarter of your book out of your head and onto paper (or a screen).

Here's how to do the writing sprints:

1. **You can't be connected to the internet. No phones. No Wi-Fi. You're not researching anything—you're writing.** You can come up with a note-taking system in case you want to go back and add a quote or some research. I use the highlighting function on Microsoft Word so these places stand out when I scan my document later.

2. **You need to know what you are going to write about.** A great outline is essential for this to work. And a little pro tip: When you sit down to do a sprint, you don't have to write your book in order. Some sections of your book will take intense thought so they may not be a good fit for a sprint. Write a story that you know well or cover an acronym or steps to accomplish something that you don't have to think hard about. Think about the examples or tips you repeat over and over again. Write that part in this sprint and you're likely to have 500 to 600 words.

3. Turn on the timer, and when it starts, do NOTHING but write. No reading. No rewriting. No pausing. **You have to keep writing, no matter what.**

4. When the timer stops, stop. Period. Take a five-minute break to stand up from your computer and then if you can, take an extra 12–15 minutes and repeat!

Imagine that if you stop writing for more than a few seconds, Pac Man is coming right up behind your words to gobble them up.

You just might find you actually do have all the time you need to write that book when you add in some of these sprints. I guarantee that if you do them enough, you'll become a more efficient writer overall.

The key to this is to not edit yourself while writing. Don't worry about little repeats or poorly written sentences. Just go. Revision can wait.

FASTER THAN THE KOENIGSEGG AGERA R

My Grandma Broad taught me from a young age that if I'm having a bad day, it's my own fault. My choices determine my outcomes. As a result, I don't need much external accountability. If I say I'm going to do something, I do it. I quickly get stressed out if I don't.

Internal motivation is the best kind. Feeling connected to a reader and knowing you MUST help them with a problem they are facing, and feeling excited about how you can do that, will fire you up on the toughest days. But if you need external motivation to keep going, find a friend or fellow writer to race to the finish line.

Join a writer's group and commit to delivering your manuscript by a certain date or you'll donate $1,000 to a charity. Hire a writing coach to hold you accountable and give them permission to call you out on your missed deadlines and push you to completion. Work with a company like Book Launchers that pushes and encourages you to achieve your goals. Write your way to massive success with one of our project managers watching your deadlines and a professional writing coach offering support.

The bottom line is, you don't have to be in a car that sputters and falters on its way to the finish line. It may never make it. Instead, jump into one of the fastest cars in the world, the Koenigsegg Agera R, put the pedal to the metal, and race to the finish line. Victory tastes so sweet.

CHAPTER 7:

GHOST-HUNTING YOUR WAY TO A BOOK

You don't think Sarah Palin,[21] Pamela Anderson,[22] Lance Armstrong,[23] and Tiffany Haddish[24] actually wrote their books, do you? Well, they didn't. Ghostwriters, in fact, have been the key to many best-selling books.

While Barack Obama reportedly writes his own books, he has pointed to the fact that his wife, Michelle, had help with her break out hit, *Becoming*.[25] Richard Branson in *Losing My Virginity* acknowledges

---

21 Alex Eichler, "What Newsweek Left Out of Its Sarah Palin Ghostwriter Profile," *The Atlantic*, April 18, 2011, https://www.theatlantic.com/culture/archive/2011/04/what-newsweek-left-out-palin-ghostwriter-profile/349731/.

22 "Pam Anderson becomes a novelist with a little help," Today, August 4, 2004, https://www.today.com/popculture/pam-anderson-becomes-novelistwith-little-help-wbna5604182.

23 David Walsh, "Embrace the anger, Sally, not the lies," *The Times*, December 16, 2012, https://www.thetimes.co.uk/article/embrace-the-anger-sally-not-the-lies-q5kjmxdk9rn.

24 Leah Rodriguez, "You'll Never Guess Who Co-Wrote Tiffany Haddish's New Memoir," *The Cut*, December 15, 2017, https://www.thecut.com/2017/12/tucker-max-co-wrote-tiffany-haddishs-new-memoir.html.

25 By Glenn Thrush and Elaina Plott, "How the Trump Campaign Is Drawing Obama Out of Retirement," *The New York Times*, June 28, 2020, https://www.nytimes.com/2020/06/28/us/politics/obama-biden-trump.html.

Edward Whitley.[26] Howard Schultz's *Onward* was penned by Joanne Gordon.[27]

Many of the top-selling books by CEOs and celebrities are penned by someone else, **but the book could not exist without the story.** The ghostwriter provides the words, and sometimes some supplemental research, but not the substance—the expertise or advice—of the pages.

That's all you, the author. So if you hate writing, don't have the time to do it, or you just know you aren't the best person for the job, hiring a talented ghostwriter could be the right choice.

A ghostwriter is someone who can write your book, in your words. Good ghostwriters work hard to capture your voice to create a first draft.

WHAT EXACTLY DOES A GHOSTWRITER DO?

The typical ghostwriting process means working with another writer to flesh out the concept for your book. You work with the writer to identify your ideal reader, develop the hook of the book, and create an outline for the book.

Using the outline, the ghostwriter will usually research the subject, collect content from the author, and then interview him/her for additional material.

At some point early on in the process, the writer will send a sample over to the author to check the tone of the writing. Then, they will get to work on the first draft.

Eventually, the writer gets feedback on the full first draft from the author and reworks the manuscript.

---

26 Richard Brandon, *Losing My Virginity: How I Survived, Had Fun, and Made a Fortune Doing Business My Way* (Australia: Currency, 2011).

27 Howard Schultz and Joanne Gordon, *Onward: How Starbucks Fought for Its Life without Losing Its Soul* (New Jersey: Wiley, 2011).

Once it's a solid draft, it's off to the editors and back to you to review and revise. Depending on your contract with your writer, you may also involve the writer in the first round of developmental edits. (I'll explain the different kinds of editors soon—you definitely want to know when to hire which kind of editor, as many authors hire the wrong editors for their needs.)

This process is the foundation for many wonderful books, but we approach ghostwriting with a slight twist at Book Launchers. We consider it more of a writing "assist." With this approach, a client begins with our Story Expert or professional Writing Coach. Typically, three to six phone calls are required to deep dive into:

- Who is your ideal reader, and what problem are you solving for them?
- How will you, the author, be defined in a unique way?
- What makes you, and the book, unique and interesting?

The hook of the book is defined, and the outline is developed based on that hook. Next, each chapter is given a short "treatment" to give the writer a foundation with which to begin.

Once all of this is complete, we're able to confidently pair our client with a writer who is skilled and experienced in their genre and is also a good personality fit. The writer is set up to succeed because the additional material he or she will need to get from conversations with the client is already fairly clear. Of course, the writer may still have to conduct some light research but a lot of the hard work is done.

The author is able to focus on providing the essential content for the book through their own writing, past content they've created, recorded interviews with the writer, or a combination of all three.

Where do you find a great ghostwriter?

Ghostwriters are everywhere. The right question really is, where do you find the right ghostwriter *for you?*

The more you know what you want, the easier it will be to identify a writer who can help you.

Here are four ideas:

1. **Ask your author friends if they have ever worked with a ghostwriter or know someone who has.**
    Many probably have not. Some may be happy to disclose they worked with a ghostwriter; others may be reluctant to share any credit for their book and say something like, "Oh, I have a friend who worked with one."

2. **Check out writing groups on LinkedIn and Facebook.**
    Many are closed groups, but if you message the administrator, you can request to join and post your query or ask them to post on your behalf. We've found some wonderful writers for our team from writing groups on social media.

3. **Search online for "business ghostwriters."**
    I connected with a few ghostwriting companies when I was looking for a ghostwriter with very specific skills for one of our clients. You can also try the Association of Ghostwriters in the US and The Writers' Union of Canada.

4. **Post a job on freelance work sites, including Guru.com, Upwork.com, Indeed.com, Reedsy, or scriptd.**
    Posting a job for a great ghostwriter may result in an overwhelming number of responses. If it does, the next question you might ask is: how do you know when you've found a good ghostwriter?

WILL WRITE FOR CHEAP—CHOOSING YOUR GHOSTWRITER

Unfortunately, I have many stories of books that have come to us after a client had a bad experience with a ghostwriter. One author found a writer on Upwork but the writer asked to move the project off Upwork because of their high fees. The author agreed, and they set a biweekly payment schedule. Everything seemed to be going okay at first but more than a year into it, the author had only received transcripts of their calls and a few written pages. He fired the writer and because he'd taken the project off Upwork, he didn't have any legal recourse to get his money back.

Another one of our clients hired a writer who pursued their own version of the author's well-known story. He struggled to get the writer to write his version of the events but, ultimately, just paid the writer for his work and brought it to us to fix. When the manuscript came to us, it was so far off the mark we had no choice but to scrap it and start over again to create the book our client wanted.

Some of these things happen because authors don't know how to effectively direct ghostwriters, or they run into trouble because they tried to cut costs. Highly experienced ghostwriters who will do a lot of research for your book typically charge $0.30–$1.00 per finished word. If they've ghostwritten *New York Times* bestsellers, they are usually on the upper end of that range.

When you understand that it will take most ghostwriters up to six months to write your book, the prices make sense. Great ghostwriters dedicate a lot of their life and time to this project. They aren't making a living if they charge much less. And it's not easy being a great ghostwriter. It's a skill to be able to write a book well and to do it in someone else's voice. They also need to be a good listener, curious, and able to ask good questions and get people to open up.

Now you can hire much cheaper writers. And the writing might even be good, but it's not just about being able to write. Being a great ghostwriter requires the ability to adapt to other voices, connect with people at a deeper, more personal level, and see the marketability and interesting angles of a book.

How do you select a great ghostwriter?

Many people think they can judge a ghostwriter by the books they've worked on. Unfortunately, not only is that not as easy as you might think but the finished book is rarely anything like the first draft produced by a ghostwriter. It's not a great way to evaluate someone.

Another challenge is that most ghostwriters have signed some sort of nondisclosure agreement and are unable to share books they have actually worked on. That makes establishing a ghostwriter's credibility a bit challenging and proof of work nearly impossible for some.

The good news is that I don't think a published book is a great way to evaluate a writer, anyway. By the time one of our books goes to print, a minimum of four other people have read and edited it. In many cases, another writer has gone in and worked through the content or provided developmental edits of the book as well, so it could be as many as five people plus the author involved in the manuscript before it's finalized.

The original writer provides the bones of the material, but the final shape of the book is driven by the entire process. This is true whether you're working with a traditional publisher or following the process of a self-publishing company like Book Launchers. If you're hiring a company like Book Launchers or working with a major publishing house, I'd focus your questions on understanding the process more than investigating the work of the writer. The quality of the process will determine the quality of your manuscript's evolution into a book.

If that's all true, how do you evaluate a ghostwriter's work?

Set yourself up for success by doing the prework before you hire someone. As noted already, you need to know your audience, your goal, and even how you want your book to be structured.

There are a lot of ways to approach this, but here's how we hire ghostwriters for the Book Launchers' team:

First, we put something in the job ad that acts as an initial screening tool.

For example, we ask a weird question in the middle of the job ad, like their favorite TV show or a fruit they don't like, or we request a writing sample in the application. If they don't follow that instruction, we immediately eliminate them. If they lack care and attention to detail when they should be showing their best self, it's not a good sign they will have it when they write.

Second, we make sure that they've worked on similar projects.

Have they written several business books before? Not just articles but full books. At Book Launchers, we get a ton of applicants for our writing positions from folks with deep nonfiction experience as journalists or bloggers but they have never written a book. Writing a full book is very different than writing articles.

A ghostwriter gets bonus points if they have written multiple books for the same company or for the same author, which speaks to the fact that they produced work that merited a continued relationship.

Third, send them a writing test.

This is the key step to ensuring that you get a ghostwriter who can capture your voice. There are a few ways to do this. You can record yourself telling a story or teaching a key point. Don't make it too long—this is a test, not a chapter. Have it transcribed using a service like rev.com or temi.com and then send that to the prospective writer. Have them turn it into a short article so you can get a sense of how they will capture your voice into words. To make this is a particularly useful test, choose something that could potentially go in your book and make sure they know your target audience.

Fourth, if we like what they wrote, we set up a time to chat.

This is essentially a personality compatibility test. A great ghostwriter should be curious about you and ready to ask questions. To get the conversation rolling, you can also ask some questions. Things we ask of potential writers include:

- *What do you love about writing nonfiction books?* We want writers who are passionate about nonfiction. Unless you want to write a fable-like nonfiction book, you probably want a nonfiction specialist who loves learning new things and translating information into material that will be helpful and easy for someone else to digest. There are people who LOVE writing nonfiction, telling fact-based stories, and really digging deep into areas they don't know about. Those are the people I want to work with.

- How do you approach a ghostwriting project? There isn't a right answer, but every effective ghostwriter has a process. If someone doesn't have any established approach at all, the responsibility for driving the process will come from an inexperienced author. A good writer should be confident and able to help even the most nervous or unorganized author come up with content.

- What's your timeline and availability for a project? Some writers will take more than a year to write a book, so it's important to consider how that is going to work for you.

- Finally, how do you prefer to communicate with a client? Make sure this is how you want to communicate as well.

If everything looks good, references are next.

Among other questions, ask references, "What was it like to work with this ghostwriter?" "What was challenging about working with them?" "What did you have to do to help them with the project?" and "What did you think about the process?"

Finally, you have to talk price and expectations. You should have a good idea of this already, from what you've read so far. But you may also want to consider:

The lower the price, the faster they need to finish a first draft. This isn't a bad thing but know that they're making money on quantity, not quality.

It's really important to know you're essentially hiring a contractor when you hire a ghostwriter. You have to manage them, set deadlines and expectations, and provide feedback. If you expect them to do research, then you need to spell that out in advance. Also, if you have extensive research and materials to be reviewed, you need to give them time to do that and explain it up front.

Remember, you're getting a manuscript, not a book.

You still have to hire one or more editors, layout designers, cover creators, and other professionals before your manuscript is a published book. The writer's job represents a first pass at getting all the words down on paper so it can be further refined and developed.

Seasoned writers won't give you a satisfaction guarantee because it sets them up for a world of pain if they get a picky client. You can set a number of rewrites or revisions in your contract but it will not be unlimited. Too many writers get burned by clients who never let the book move on to editing. Even if a writer promises two or three revisions, you will have to hire more help.

Also, to ensure you get the book you actually want, read early chapters and check in with the ghostwriter as chapters are done to be confident your book hasn't veered off course. It's your job to manage the process from the start to make sure you get what you want.

TIPS TO EFFECTIVELY CARE AND FEED YOUR GHOSTWRITER TO GET THE BEST WORK

Ghostwriting can go wrong in many ways, but most of the problems are preventable by following the previous guidelines. Here are a few other tips to help you get the most out of your ghostwriter:

1. Be clear on your concept before you make the hire. Some ghostwriters can help you flesh out your ideas but you can expect to pay a lot more for that work. Ultimately, it's your job to create the concept and have a plan for how the book will flow.

2. You need to help your writer capture your voice through conversations and by providing written, oral materials, or videos. The more they are immersed in your voice, the easier it will be for them to write like you would write.

3. Plan to speak to the ghostwriter once a week for about 60–90 minutes. Any more than that and the writer won't have time to digest everything and put it into writing; any less and it's hard for the writer to stay connected to you and the project. Leaving your ghostwriter to work on your book for weeks at a time can create a disconnect.

4. Review all the chapters carefully but pay especially close attention to the first few chapters. Make sure your voice can be heard and you are happy with the tone of the book. You don't need to nitpick individual word choices, but you do need to make sure the book is following your plan and sounds like you. If you see issues with the work early on, address it. Don't think it will get better or worry about hurting your writer's feelings. It's going to be a lot worse if you get halfway or to the end and then tell your writer you're unhappy. Be upfront about any concerns you have as soon as you have them.

5. The first pass is not going to be perfect so give the writer room to breathe. Make sure the key elements of your stories, lessons,

and ideas are presented and you can hear your voice in the words but don't worry about spelling or grammar errors. Remember, you're getting a manuscript and the book is developed through many iterations of future editing. Some authors ride the ghostwriters so hard about making every sentence perfect that the writer loses their ability to write because they struggle to meet those expectations. There is a balance between giving the writer feedback to get your first draft where you want it and making sure the writer is motivated to keep going. Which leads me to the next point:

6. Your writer is a human being. Being a professional writer doesn't mean you suddenly aren't afraid of being bad at what you do. Treat them like you would any other person. Give them input and feedback on areas where they can improve, and let them know what they are doing that you really think is great. Sure, it's your book, but that doesn't give you license to be a total jerk about it. Thank them, celebrate them, and be sure to tell them when they are writing something you think is great. It's the decent thing to do. If you want the best work out of anyone, you should be celebrating the things they are doing right more than you're pointing out all the things they need to improve.

One final note about working with a writer: you need to check your ego for your book to be a success.

We often have clients who come in and demand a "technical writer" or someone with "scientific or medical" expertise. They want their book to be respected in their field and demand someone who understands all the fancy industry terminology. That is a fair expectation and request if your audience is limited to colleagues in your industry or you have an academic audience.

Most of the time, these authors want their book to be a bestseller and widely read. If you want your book to be widely read, you don't want it full of industry jargon. A perfect example of the kind of writing you need can be found in *Wired*. The magazine's writers cover extremely technical subjects like the biomechanics of athletes, electric car manufacturing, space travel, and more. And they do it in a way that is interesting and easy to read. They speak to an intelligent reader but not someone who necessarily requires a PhD to connect with the message and learn from the article.

Using big words unnecessarily and making complex ideas even more difficult to understand by wrapping it in fancy language is the quickest way to exclude the majority of readers. You may want a writer who is comfortable with your field but isn't an expert. They know enough to ask thoughtful questions but not so much they miss explaining things that the average person would need to understand something.

One of our recent clients was horrified that a ghostwriter used simplistic terms to connect ideas instead of "henceforth" and "furthermore." At the same time, she expected the book to connect with the general population. She felt excluding those words dumbed her down, and because she had a PhD and wanted her academic colleagues to respect her work, she was unrelenting.

In the end, it was her book so we did what she wanted, but she's going to have a challenge connecting to her ideal reader. Good writing is not complicated or fancy.

Good writing makes a reader turn pages and rave about what they just learned. Remember that, whether you've hired a writer or you're writing your own book. It's not about sounding smart, it's about communicating well. Above all, connect with your reader.

CHAPTER 8:

PSSST...I KNOW WHY YOU HAVEN'T WRITTEN YOUR BOOK YET

"I fear you're making a big mistake. Everyone in LA gets divorced and does drugs."

The woman I often consider my greatest inspiration in life wrote that to me in a four-page letter after I told her I was leaving Canada and moving to the United States. My late and dear Grandma Broad, the woman who taught me it's my own fault if I have a bad day. She was trying to convince me not to pack up my newborn son and husband and head south.

At 40, I was making a radical change to support my husband's dream. But in my heart, I knew it was the right change for me too. California was calling.

Her letter shocked and hurt me.

I figured if I could count on anyone's support, it would be my always-positive, strong Grandma.

You probably have someone like my Grandma Broad in your life telling you not to write your book. They care and are probably trying to keep you safe, in their own way. Unfortunately, that advice only keeps you small. Nobody ever made a great impact on the world playing it safe.

You may have heard things like this as you've set out to write your book:

- Aren't you busy enough? Nobody makes money selling books—you're wasting your time.
- Why should you write a book?
- You don't want to put your dirty laundry out for the world to see!
- You can barely type. How do you think you're going to write a book?

Take comments like these for what they are: the fears of others projected onto you.

Rarely will such negativity come from high achievers (unless they're jealous). Those people are too busy making things happen in their own lives to worry about what you're doing.

The naysayers and critics aren't the real issue holding you back from having a gigantic impact on others, though.

Your biggest obstacle to becoming an author is much, much harder to ignore.

THE BIGGEST ENEMY YOU FACE IN WRITING A GREAT BOOK

When you start putting pen to paper, the question arises: Who are you to write a book? The answer can your biggest threat—clearly, an imposter.

It makes sense. A book is a proven way to become a known authority, boost your business, and give you a public profile. When you get close to achieving that kind of success, all kinds of freaky demons bubble up from within:

- Am I worthy?
- Maybe I got to where I am because of luck.
- It's easy for me, so maybe it's easy for everyone, and I'm not special or different in any way.
- No one needs me or my book.

Fear of what other people will think and insecurity around your expertise and experience rush in. Suddenly, a book seems like the wrong move.

Know that almost everyone suffers from "imposter syndrome" when they write a book. Or perform on stage, for that matter. It's normal, and it's probably good. It means you'll work that much harder to produce something that matters to your readers. It also makes it more likely you'll bring on the professionals required to make your book the best it can be.

If you start feeling this, think back to the goal you have for your reader. Remember how your book is going to make your reader's life better and reconnect to your hook. That should get you reinvigorated.

When you write the book that needs to be written, not the one that you think will make you look good, you can fight the Resistance a little easier. But you still have to decide what goes in the book.

PUT IT IN THE BIN OR IN THE BOOK?

If you have a story that isn't directly relevant to your subject, how much of it should you include in your book? How much detail should you go into?

The answer isn't a simple formula but it comes down to this:

What does the reader need to know?

The book isn't for you. It's for your reader. Many people treat writing a book like therapy—and the reality is that it IS therapeutic to write down your story. It's also true that nobody, not even your best friend or your own mother, wants every detail.

Defining moments in your life were hard. They shaped who you are. Those moments are important to share; however, readers need only the essentials to learn the lessons relevant to them.

Robin Sharma, the best-selling Canadian author, addresses this beautifully.

"Leave your ego at the door every morning, and just do some truly great work," he says. "Few things will make you feel better than a job brilliantly done."

Focus on whom you are helping with your book and why.

Then get someone with an outside perspective who understands your goals to read your book.

Notice the important words in that sentence? Outside perspective.

Your spouse, brother, friend, or even your cousin all know you. They will likely find your stories more interesting because of that. They are also likely to be kinder than they should be about your work. The truth is that the input you need for your book will hurt a little. It reminds me of when my writing coach said, "That was a great story, but why did you make me read it?"

It was a good story, but it didn't serve a purpose for my reader nor did it align with the hook, the promise of my book.

Remember, it's not about whether something is interesting, useful, or entertaining. Run every decision of whether to bin (throw out) or book (keep) something through this simple filter:

- Does this support the hook of my book?
- Is this something that needs to be shared in order to achieve the promise of the book?
- Who benefits the most from this section? If the answer isn't the reader, you know where to put it.

If you're really not sure, that's where a great book writing coach comes in.

THE AUTHOR'S SECRET WEAPON

What is a writing coach, also called a book coach, and how does this person help you?

The role varies a little bit client by client because everybody has different needs, but at Book Launchers, a writing coach always:

- Offers emotional support through the book writing journey.
- Provides a writing plan, deadlines, and accountability.
- Guides the author to write in a more engaging, interesting, and (hopefully) concise way to connect to their ideal reader.

Generally speaking, if you haven't already established the foundation for your book (audience, hook, and outline), that will be the first work you do with a book coach.

More specifically, we expect our writing coaches to help authors:

1. **Build audience clarity:** A great writing coach will work with the author to really understand the reader at an emotional level, what's likely happening in their life right now, and most important, problems the author can solve for them. This is essential. In other words, the coach helps an author figure out who their book is helping and how.

2. **Develop the hook:** The juicy thing that you are uniquely suited to offer a very specific reader can be hard for you to see for yourself. It has to be benefit-driven, create curiosity, and make

your ideal reader pay attention—that can be hard to spot on your own, and it may take multiple conversations with a great writing coach to figure out.

3. **Draft an outline:** Usually we get an author to brainstorm every subject they can think of for their book. Then, with the writing coach, they organize it into major points and sub points to be covered, evaluating each one according to the criteria of whether it fits with their hook. A professional eye not only provides guidance but keeps an author's eye on the ball.

4. **Create a writing plan:** Will you write a chapter a week? Will you set a word count goal? Or will you just see what you can accomplish in a two-hour writing session? My recommended approach to our clients is to set a standing appointment each week with the writing coach and commit to what you'll write before the next call. Coaches will use that time to hold the author accountable, review what has been written, and agree on a plan for the next week.

5. **Write a first chapter template:** For first-time authors, writing a chapter can feel a bit foreign, and while chapters don't need to be the same length, a book works best with some consistent structure. The writing coach will work closely with the author to develop the first chapter to use as a model for the rest of the book.

6. **Provide writing guidance:** Typically, writing coaches and editors give instructions like "expand on this" or "add some emotion," which can seem daunting and vague to a novice writer. Writing coaches aren't writers (or at least they aren't playing the role of a writer when you hire them as a coach). But it's fair for a coach to write out a section as an example or a teaching point. Sometimes a novice writer needs to see it and then they can apply a similar approach going forward. We also encourage our writing coaches to help our clients avoid passive voice

(more on that in a minute), start chapters in an interesting way, and add stories and examples to create engagement with the reader.

7. **Offer emotional support:** A book is a big project and it can be lonely. A writing coach will provide some emotional support as you ride the inevitable waves of confidence (my book will sell millions of copies) and insecurity (my book sucks). They also will keep you focused, especially since it's easy for nonfiction authors to lose track of their hook and start writing an entirely different book halfway through!

8. **Take names and kick butt:** We often joke that being a great writing coach requires a psychology background. You have to be able to ask personal questions of authors to get to the heart of what makes someone awesome and interesting. You also need to be able to be supportive while pushing them to get it done, even if it's not perfect. A great coach makes it okay to write a bad first draft before you have a polished diamond of a book.

9. **Keep the book interesting and in line with the hook:** Most authors start off strong then veer off course into boring territory. Some authors start writing a totally different book part way through the process. A book coach can stop an author from adding unnecessary or irrelevant details (yes, I'm looking at you, Ms. or Mr. Memoir author—more for you in a moment) or help the author impart more emotion to the manuscript. A great writing coach is watching for this and is going to hit pause and dig into things a little to help you share stories that keep the reader glued to the page.

Whew, I bet you had no idea how much work a writing coach does to make your book great.

Did you notice what a writing coach does *not* do, though? A writing coach does not edit your book, and while they may write example sections so you understand how to craft certain things in your book, they are not writing your book for you either.

Your coach is there to make sure your first draft is the best possible first draft. And the value in that is enormous.

One of our clients spoke to me a year before engaging with us, and he said he'd write his book and then bring it to us for editing. I said sure, go ahead, but your book will be better if you work with our writing coach to develop it first.

"I'm very confident with what I'm writing and that it will be marketable," he said. "I just need to get the draft done so you can edit it."

A year later, he brought us the draft, and while there was some great content in there, the hook was weak and some of the content irrelevant. The entire book needed to be reworked, and we worked through the process of tearing his book apart to build it back up. He may have saved the expense of hiring a book coach but he wasn't spared the emotional pain.

"I guess this is a little like calling you in to fix a house that wasn't built right to begin with," he said, reflecting on his experience. "You have to take it down to the studs to get it right."

Not everyone needs a book coach or a writing coach but most authors would benefit from one.

It's a lonely process writing a book, and sometimes, more than anything, it's nice to know you're not in it alone.

WHAT TO LOOK FOR IN YOUR BOOK COACH

Some of our clients, especially authors with technical or financial expertise, insist on finding a book coach who is just like them because they will better understand them. This is only advisable if your ideal reader is just like you too. But if your ideal readers aren't like you and won't understand you, then who you really want is a book coach more like your reader. Think carefully about what is important to appeal to your ideal reader and find someone who can reinforce your strengths, not your weaknesses.

Based on my experience hiring writing coaches and watching what works (and what doesn't always work), I recommend you look for:

1. Someone with experience writing nonfiction books. Ideally, they've written more than one. You'll find ghostwriters can make great book coaches because they understand what it takes to write a book, capture someone's voice, and get to the heart of what someone is trying to communicate.

2. A personality fit. Being best friends isn't what you need, but you do want someone with whom you feel comfortable because you'll communicate a lot.

3. Skills that balance your strengths. If you are a very analytical person, you should find a writing coach who will help you bring some emotional balance to your work. If you're highly emotional and creative, you may want a writing coach with structure and discipline to ensure your book flows and is backed up with enough data to be credible.

4. Someone with the confidence and experience to tell you what can make your book better. One of our clients worked with a writing coach before she signed up with us. "I felt like she was more like a cheerleader telling me how good the book was and encouraging me to go on. The feedback was good for my ego but it wasn't constructive or really useful," she said. "Your writing coach gives me in-depth comments that are really making this a better book."

5. A different background than you. Some of our clients hire writing coaches and editors from their industry, thinking that

someone needs to understand their topic to give them good feedback. There's value in having someone "in the know" work on your book, but what is even more important is having someone who comes at your book from a totally different background and viewpoint. What will make your book stand out is a new perspective on the things everyone in your industry already knows.

Bonus points: Storytelling experience. From screenplays to books and comedy skits to speeches, I like to find writing coaches who can help clients wield influence with their words and tell a great story. It can be a great asset for your book to find someone who can help you shape a narrative that will grab and keep an audience's attention. The ability to tell a great story can be taught but it's an uncommon natural skill.

THREE MISTAKES WRITING YOUR MEMOIR— DON'T WRITE A BOOK NOBODY READS!

Memoirs can be a great way to share experiences, help others see they aren't alone in their struggles, and pass on stories from generation to generation but memoirs are very challenging to market. Some authors write a memoir for legacy and that is great. Your memoir might be the greatest gift to give family members for decades to come.

You are brave and courageous to share your story. And your story matters.

But even memoirs with incredible stories are hard to sell if you aren't famous.

Please don't let me deter you. The following tips are intended to help you create a book that is more marketable if selling your memoir is important to you.

Mistake one is writing your story but not writing a story that the reader will enjoy.

First, read this:

"I grew up in a house attached to a 20-room motel that was built on the side of Highway 1 in Alberta, Canada. I had one brother. When I was a teenager, my parents took in another kid, giving me a second brother. My parents worked hard at the motel and never really got a break from work. It was a seven-day-a-week, 24-hours-a-day job. My dad would have to answer the door at all hours. Sometimes that was scary. But I liked seeing the business operate. It influenced me to start my own business later in life."

Typical memoir.

Now try this on for size:

"It was 2:00 a.m. and I heard the doorbell ring. I peeked out my bedroom door to see my dad wearing a housecoat and carrying a baseball bat as he walked down the stairs. It always scared me to see this, but my parents owned and operated a 20-room motel on the side of the highway. The doorbell was almost always someone asking for a room, but my dad had faced a few scary people at that hour, so he brought a bat just in case. It wasn't easy living attached to the motel, but it provided an incredible education about what it's like to own and operate your own business."

Okay, which book do you want to read? They're both something I could have written, but the first one is what most memoir writers do. They sit down and they write their story in a linear fashion in what is known among writers as an "exposition draft." They focus on themselves and start at the beginning. In the second version, the author writes the story for the reader focusing on grabbing their attention and creating a dramatic narrative.

Write for your reader. They don't need every detail but they do need a good story.

The second mistake is telling your story in chronological order.

The typical three-act structure divides a story into three parts.

Act I is the Set Up, the inciting incident. It's the thing that sets you off on your adventure. For Alice in *Alice in Wonderland*, it's curiosity and the thrill of the chase that sends her off on her adventure. Another classic is Alec Baldwin's speech in the film *Glengarry Glen Ross*, when he says, "Sell or be fired. Always Be Closing."

Basically, it's a call to adventure that leads up to Act II.

Act II is the Confrontation, where things get intense. It's often the midpoint, but generally it's when a lot of things pile on top of each other and create a conflict with an obstacle(s) that seems insurmountable.

And then comes Act III, the resolution and lead up to the climax and the denouement.

Remember, it's not about telling the story in chronological order! It's about layering in story structure.

A memoir by definition is a historical account or biography. It's a book about your life and the lessons you want to pass on. It's not simply a retelling of your history or a book-length diary. It's not "an exposition draft."

You can skip days, months, even years in your story. And you do not need to tell it in order for it to make sense to a reader.

Most people don't understand story arcs, and the author is often too close to their story to see what adds value to their story and what doesn't. That's why writing coaches are so valuable.

Finally, the third mistake is forgetting about the benefit to the reader.

Most memoir authors tell me they want to "inspire others just like them." That's very common but inspiration is actually tough to market.

You went to jail for a crime you didn't commit. A powerful story but what's the lesson? What does a reader take away from that?

Your brother-in-law turns out to be a serial killer. Wow. Incredible. But what is the lesson? This is an actual example of a book we worked on, by the way—*Killers Keep Secrets: The Golden State Killers Other Life* by James Huddle. The lesson is really about how you don't always know the people closest to you and what to watch out for.

In another example, Nelson Tressler was the center of the biggest trial ever to hit his small town—as a newborn baby. Imagine being the focus of rape and murder charges from the start of your life. His story is fascinating but it would have been hard to market had it not been layered with the lessons he learned. He shares how readers can turn early despair into a life with a loving family and a multi-million-dollar business empire. (Definitely check this one out if you want to learn how to succeed when you start at the bottom—*The Unlucky Sperm Club: You are Not a Victim of Your Circumstances but a Product of Your Choices*.)

What is the emotional journey for your reader, and what do you hope they get from your story? Why should they read your book and recommend it to others?

Think about how you want your reader to fill in the blank:

This was such a good book. This story taught me _____.

You might have an incredible tale but without this core message, you don't really have a book.

You are brave and generous for wanting to share your story with others. Just be sure that you know your reader and what they need to know so your message gets across to them and serves your desired purpose.

CHAPTER 9:

THE UNEXPECTED PROBLEM WITH BOOK EDITORS

Want to know something nobody tells you? The first draft of your book is supposed to be lousy! That's right. When have you EVER done something major and been amazing at it the first try?

Did you ever pick up a golf club for the first time and magically make a hole-in-one? If you learned a new language, were you able to converse fluently the first day? What about learning to play an instrument? Were you able to play your first song after one lesson?

Of course not.

The first time I tried to do the butterfly stroke in swimming, I bet the lifeguard was getting ready to dive in after me.

Tell me why, then, you think your book should be perfect on the first pass?

The first order of business is creating a bad first draft. Once you've got that, you have material to work on so that your book can be good and then great. Plus, if you've done the work around getting clear on your audience and developing a hook, your book is on a solid foundation. The rest is just words on the page.

And once you have pages, it's time to call in the most important people you'll have on your manuscript production team—editors!

DIFFERENT KINDS OF EDITORS, AND WHAT YOU ACTUALLY NEED

Editors go by many names: Substantive editors, developmental editors, content editors, copy editors, and proofreaders. What do all these editors do, and how can they make your book the best it can be?

Substantive editing, also called *developmental editing* or even *comprehensive editing*, is where the editor looks at the overall concept of your book and evaluates it against its intended use or goal. The editor really is looking at the book from a high level to evaluate the organization and writing style. At Book Launchers, we call this content editing.

The Role of a Content Editor

The purpose of a content editor is to make the document functional for its readers. There's always an element of cutting out stuff you don't need and adding more to areas that aren't as clear or need more explanation. Most content editors will ask for your sources.[28]

Our goal at Book Launchers is a little broader than a typical content edit. We want your book to be entertaining and engaging for the reader. Nobody likes reading textbooks. The best books are almost

---

28 Podcasters, it's worth noting here that you should be getting every single person you interview on your podcast to sign a legal waiver in case you want to use that interview for your book in the future. This saves you time so you don't have to chase them down later.

always the ones that entertain while educating. We attempt to edit to create engagement.

We also consider to whom you are marketing your book and whether your work connects with that target market. Are you likely to achieve your desired outcome from this manuscript?

Content editors at Book Launchers make recommendations to help you ensure you've set yourself up to sell your services or attract leads. For example, if you're building a speaking business, have you mentioned a few talks you've given in your book? Have you seeded the outcome for folks who hire you for consulting gigs, or have you showcased what your product or service can do in at least one story? We also look for opportunities to create lead magnets and content for placement in magazines and blogs.

Content editing is almost entirely analysis based. It's not what most people think is involved in editing someone's book. It's less about correcting grammar and punctuation and more about moving parts around, looking at the language used to explain things, and ensuring that ideas are presented clearly and logically.

It's also the worst phase of editing for most authors. Almost always, the manuscript is returned to the author with a lot of questions to answer, research to add, or sources to site. It's tough because you probably feel like your book is mostly done and then the content edit comes back and you realize you still have a lot of work to do.

I recommend you prepare yourself mentally for this edit. It can hit some authors pretty hard. It's discouraging and disappointing, but it's probably the most important part of working on a book. **It's where your good book becomes great.**

You can take or leave the editorial suggestions. The goal is to make decisions and revisions that improve your book and make sure your reader gets the desired outcome.

A Copy Editor Has a Different but Equally Important Role

Copy editing is VERY different than content editing. At Book Launchers, we hire different people for each job because it's a different skill set. Copy editing is more rules-based and focuses on grammar, commas and punctuation, mechanics of style, and consistency in how things are presented. While your document may come back with a lot of red on it, it's usually much easier to process and work through your copy-edited manuscript. It's more a matter of accepting sentence changes, approving the addition of a few hundred commas, and reviewing any other recommended wording changes.

At this point, you've done the heavy lifting of really thinking through the message, flow, and impact of your book and now you're focused on refining it.

We typically put books through two rounds of copy edits in order to get the manuscript to an almost final draft. This allows the book to be improved and then polished. The goal is that, after the first round of copy edits, you're done adding to the book and now it's all about refinement.

Of course, that is the goal but that's not always what happens.

The Final Editor on Your Team—the Proofreader

The final set of eyes you want on your manuscript is a proofreader. This IS a role you can give to that nitpicky relative or your aunt who taught university. While I wouldn't recommend using anybody but a professional copy editor for the copy editing, proofreading can be crowdsourced or sent to a hawk-eyed friend who knows APA Style rules. Whoever you hire or get to do this, their job is to catch the final little things that are left over. Are words consistently hyphenated? Is capitalization done properly? Are there any sneaky little typos that have been overlooked?

The goal is to get to an error-free document, but that's not easily achieved. The proofreader provides a fresh set of eyes to catch superficial errors in spelling, grammar, syntax, punctuation, and formatting. This is the editor who prevents Amazon reviewers from pointing out "all the errors" when only a couple of typos snuck in...but they snuck in.

The bottom line is, most authors need a content editor, proofreader, and copy editor. If you're an experienced writer with a good book outline, you may be able to get away with a copy editor who does a little more work on your book than usual, but generally your book needs all three.

DON'T WASTE YOUR MONEY ON THE WRONG EDITOR

"My editor made the book grammatically correct, but she didn't make it better!"

Too many authors submit edited manuscripts thinking the book is ready to publish when it's not, or they're wondering why their book is still not good after thousands of dollars spent on editing. What's gone wrong?

All authors—100 percent—need editors. All professional writers—100 percent—need editors. In fact, most authors and writers need more than one editor.

You CANNOT edit your own work. Your brain plays tricks on you, and you'll only see how something is supposed to be written, not how it's actually written.

However, you can take several steps to make sure your book is in relatively good condition before you pay the professionals. We'll talk about self-editing tips in a second, but first here are the three most common ways I see editing situations go wrong for well-intentioned authors.

1. You hire an editor but your book really needs someone who will help you further develop the idea.

    Editors are not the same as writing coaches and hiring an editor before your book is fully developed is a mistake.

    If you're not really sure where your book stands in terms of development, ask a few colleagues or friends to read it (beta readers—*more on them in a minute*). Then, ask them to answer a few questions such as:

    - What do you think this book is about?
    - What kind of person will read it?
    - What will they learn from it?
    - What would you change?

    If your beta readers are coming back with positive and consistent answers to these questions, then you're probably ready for editing.

2. You hired an editor but you weren't clear on what you expected in terms of editing results.

    If you hire a copy editor—you're going to get a copy edit.

    Some great copy editors will flag areas of your book that need improvement, but their job is to follow a list of rules and make sure your book follows those rules.

3. You hired an editor without checking their experience.

    Every two to three months, we bring on at least one new editor to the Book Launchers team. When we open up the hiring process, we usually get as many as 100 applicants in a few days.

    Of those, only about 15–20 percent are actually professional editors.

Many people say they have a great eye for mistakes, but they base that on the fact that they edited web content at their job or they've edited some academic papers. That's not professional editing.

You want someone who eats, sleeps, and breathes editing.

If they haven't edited a bunch of other books in your genre (nonfiction, ideally business books or memoirs), move on.

One quick check is to visit their LinkedIn page. If they cite editing as their main occupation, you're starting off with a good foundation. Check if they are a member of an editing association or they have taken training. Ask for references. Be certain they are making their living as an editor before you hire them to edit your book.

TIPS FOR EDITING YOUR OWN BOOK

Before you read this, please know that what I am about to suggest is NOT a substitute for hiring professional editors. This is IN ADDITION to professional editors.

You can improve your book, ultimately saving money and time, by using the correct self-editing techniques and allotting appropriate time for the process. Here are five tips for self-editing success:

1. **Don't edit while you write.**
   Do you spend more time editing than writing? You're wasting time! Have a plan, write the stories, tips, and tactics you need to share. If something seems off while you write, reread and make content additions and adjustments if you must, but remember your ONLY goal once you start writing is to WRITE! There's nothing to edit if you don't write the book.

2. **After your first draft is done...set it aside for AT LEAST ONE week. You need space and probably a break.**

When you pick it back up, read it from start to finish and ask yourself three simple questions:

- Is everything there?
- What can I cut?
- Do I start the book in a REALLY compelling way for the reader?

    Can I deliver more value earlier in the book?

    Does everything fit with the hook of the book?

Once you feel like you've got everything written, you're ready for a developmental editor or content editor.

3. **Edit sentence by sentence.**
    This is as monotonous as it sounds. I do this when the book comes back from copy editing, and I use the copy editor as my guide for where I need to spend more time. For the record, this is also when I begin to hate every single book I've written. Details are not my thing, and this essential editing step is painful for me. You may enjoy it. This is where a book goes from good to great so it's important. As you go through your book sentence by sentence, here's your task list:

    - Cut anything that is not absolutely necessary. Fluffy words. Repetitive sentences.
    - Look at sentences that start with "I" and ask yourself if you can speak more directly to the reader.
    - Change passive sentences to active sentences (this goes for verbs too) and be more direct whenever you can (more on this in the next chapter because active writing is the foundation of a #noboringbooks approach to writing!).
    - Question the use of "big words." Do you need them or can you simplify the language?
    - Are you using industry JARGON or just common fluffy phrases? You know, are you saying something like, **"This**

out-of-the-box thinking is good but let's circle back and touch base later to do a deep dive and create some action items to defeat the 800-pound-gorilla."

- Does anything date the book? Are you okay with that? Can you reword it?
- Then, of course, review word choices and issues flagged by the copy editor.

Once you get this painful part done, you're on the home stretch and things get way more fun! ☺

4. **Read it aloud.**

Reading your book aloud and making sure every sentence reads well and makes sense is a powerful editing tool. For whatever reason, you also are more likely to discover typos than when you read silently. I recommend doing this after a proofread and before it goes to layout. It's just a great way to catch little things! If you're recording an audiobook, this is going to happen, anyway.

5. **STOP EDITING**

What? A self-editing tip that tells you to stop editing? We've seen authors fall into a cycle of never-ending edits, when they are no longer making their book better and are simply stalling.

Every single book is published with a mistake, or three. You won't find them all, and the more you meddle with your book, the more mistakes you introduce. This is a FACT!

Plus, every editor you hire is going to find issues. That's their job. Have you ever had a property inspector come out of a house and tell you it was perfect? Nope. Never happens. I've been involved in nearly 100 real estate transactions and every property had a list of problems—even brand new properties. We had to decide what issues required fixing and which were okay to leave. You need to do the same with your book.

WHAT DOES ALL THIS EDITORIAL GENIUS COST?

The Editorial Freelance Association keeps a pretty good working chart on what you can expect to pay for different editors. (Check it out: https://www.the-efa.org/rates/.)

Content editing can depend on how much work needs to be done, so it's best to submit a sample and get a quote.

Generally, you can expect to pay roughly $30–$60/hour for copy editing. The expectation is that a copy editor will edit somewhere around 500–1,250 words per hour. The range will vary based on the experience of the editor and the quality of the manuscript. If it hasn't had any editing yet, you can expect to pay on the higher end of that range. If your work has gone through a professional content editor or you've had some diligent and savvy beta readers, the fee will likely be on the lower end of that price range.

Finally, proofreading is typically priced out by the word. About 0.005 to 0.01 cent per word is pretty standard but check for the latest prices because industry norms fluctuate.

DO YOU HAVE YOUR FACTS STRAIGHT?

Authors, we have a responsibility. People may be using your work as a reference for their work. For years and years to come, your book could be quoted over and over. Wouldn't it be embarrassing and potentially liability-creating to discover that something you put in your book was wrong? You're writing this book to establish your credibility, right?

Books have always seemed like a very trustworthy source of information. I'd always assumed there was a very rigorous fact-checking process for every nonfiction book, which meant I could count on what I was reading to be true. It turns out that isn't the case.

In fact, it's more common for a book to skip the fact-checking process[29] than it is for it to go through it. That's largely because, in both traditionally published books and self-published books, fact-checking will happen only at the author's expense.

The cost of an error is fairly low for a publisher so most don't think it's worth the expense. In a world where people are telling lies to support their agenda, that is a pretty unsettling thought.

Here's the most important thing for authors though: Just because an error may not cost you big financially, it could cost YOUR reputation. As an author, especially one writing a book to build credibility, grow your influence, and add to your income, you want to establish yourself as an authority by being right!

If you're like me and details aren't your thing or you're just crazy busy, you should hire the professionals to help you. A fact-checker will look at any sentences where you make claims and say, "Where's the proof?"

Specifically, a fact-checker will:

1. Review the quality of sources that you've used and find primary sources if possible. Primary sources are the original source of information. That means not using Wikipedia! A fact-checker will look for the original research, firsthand account of someone who was actually there or involved, interview transcripts, or the original source of the statistical data. Secondary sources will then be found if primary sources aren't available. Secondary sources are based on that primary source usually but they have commentary or other material or interpretations included. This is what you find in journals and articles, reviews and books.

---

29 https://www.theatlantic.com/entertainment/archive/2014/09/why-books-still-arent-fact-checked/378789/

2. Make sure that everything that needs to be verified is verified. They go through and ask, "Is that really true?" A good fact-checker is going to question assumptions and ask, "Who said it? How do they know? What was their expertise related to that claim? Can this claim be corroborated by a trustworthy source?"

3. Make sure all the sources are properly formatted and tidied into footnotes and endnotes for your peace of mind and easy reference, should anyone question the authenticity of your claims.

It's a really good idea to bring in fact-checkers for your book, if you have a lot of research, state a lot of things like their facts when they might not be, or you've also said a lot of things that aren't fully verified.

FINDING GREAT EDITORS

Now that you know what kind of editor you need for your book, here's how to find what you need:

Search the internet.

You can review sites like Reedsy.com, Guru.com, UpWork.com, seek referrals on Facebook or LinkedIn, or go through an editorial association such as the National Association of Independent Writers and Editors or The Society for Editing in the US or the Editors' Association of Canada. Editors are everywhere. You just have to know what you're looking for!

Filter the results.

In my experience, it helps to:

1. Look for someone who works full time as an editor.

2. Find an editor with experience in your category. While a proof-reader doesn't have to be genre specific, it's useful to have a developmental/substantive and.or a copy editor who is experienced with your kind of book. At Book Launchers, we've encountered situations where it's important to have an editor who is familiar with the language used during a certain time period. For example, we had a client whose book was set during World War II in England. We hired an editor whose background allowed her to make the time-appropriate choices and suggestions.

Once you get a list of five editors, send an email to briefly introduce yourself and your project. Give them a sense of the word or page count and your timeline, which helps them assess their availability.

We typically give our editors about two weeks to work on a manuscript before they return it to our clients. If it's more than 65,000 words, we extend that timeline by up to a week.

When you're considering a timeline, remember you need to have time yourself to go through the edits. Most of our clients will move through the copy edit fairly quickly but developmental editing can take a month or longer for the author to process and revise the manuscript. Give yourself more time than you think you'll need. Unless you're really confident in your writing skills, you'll probably find many areas that need development and revisions.

Once you hear back from the editors, send an editing test to those who are interested in your project. Consider sending each of them the same two pages from your manuscript so they can get a sense of your work and edit it for your review. This also makes it easier to compare candidates for the same editing role.

Next, evaluate the tests. Depending on the type of editing, your review will vary. If you're screening content editors, for instance, you want to see suggestions about how to add humor, make something much more interesting or easier to understand, add credibility, improve the flow of the document, and note where sources, examples, or stories should be added.

Some editors are very opinionated, and you may or may not appreciate their comments. Listen to your gut when you read what they've done. Our clients are not professional writers so they need a mix of encouragement and suggestions. Still, edits should be provided in as objective a manner as possible.

If you're hiring for a copy edit, consider which candidate caught the greatest number of errors. We use a feature on Microsoft Word to merge and compare documents that allows us to see who is catching more issues and making revisions for improved comprehension or clarity.

As a final check, ask yourself if you think you're going to get along with this person, or not. If there's a clear winner, go with them unless their pricing exceeds your budget. In general, though, if you can find a fantastic editor, they're probably worth the higher cost.

WHAT IS A BETA READER?

Beta readers are introduced at different stages of the book process: first draft, mid-edit, and prepublication. Each phase has a different objective.

What can be done to address the flaws or weak areas of the book? Beta readers can be a great resource at this stage if you haven't worked with a writing coach or had anybody look at your book. This is also a great place to get input from people who fall into your ideal reader category or people who know your ideal reader really well.

Mid-edit, beta reading is more about catching smaller issues, such as how things are explained and whether the book keeps the audience engaged from page to page and chapter to chapter.

Final draft use of a beta reader gives you an extra set of eyes to catch any errors before your book goes to print. The beta reader can also give you a boost of confidence that your book is good enough to publish. A beta reader at this stage also can serve the double purpose of being an early reviewer or early supporter of your book.

Some people recommend working ONLY with other writers while others suggest your beta readers should be selected from your target audience. I think it depends on the kind of feedback you seek and your desired outcome.

Determining the goal of a beta reader(s) is your first task, if you think this is a route you want to take. What is the point of using a beta reader? Spell it out. Do you want a pair of eagle eyes to look for errors in your manuscript before you sign off on it? Or do you want to know where your book may be dull or confusing for your targeted audience?

Write that down so you are clear. I give our beta readers instructions in the form of questions so I can be sure we're getting the input we need.

For instance, we've asked beta readers who are testing client books:

1. What do you think the book is about?

2. Who do YOU think is the most likely audience for the book?

3. What do you like about the book?

4. If you could change something about the book, what would you change?

When we bring on beta readers for client books, we don't want editing because we have a team of professionals. We're usually trying to have other people point out the problems in a book that we've been trying to fix and our author is resisting fixing. We'll usually give beta readers a two-week turnaround, noting we don't expect they will have read the book word for word, cover to cover.

When it comes to nonfiction, it's generally best to go with people who represent your target audience. Fellow writers in a similar space can be invaluable too.

A word of caution: When I used beta readers for my previous books, I found that only 20 percent actually finished reading the book even though I gave them a month. People have good intentions but mediocre follow-through. Know that going in. If you want five opinions, ask 15–20 people!

Finally, while beta readers are rarely paid for their service, it's still a service, so I recommend showing your appreciation in the form of a token fee, gift card, or service in kind. If they took the time and effort to provide you with decent input, that deserves a thank you. At the very least, send them a nice thank you note and a copy of your book when it comes out!

That said, I'm generally not a fan of beta readers. Here's why:

1. Beta readers have the best of intentions but intentions don't always translate into clear, actionable advice to improve your book.

2. The process of using beta readers slows down your book with minimal added value in many cases.

3. You can become overconfident or overly critical of your book after getting feedback from the beta readers. We have a lot of authors who bring us manuscripts with glowing feedback from their early readers. We read it and wonder who the heck was telling this lovely person such falsehoods. Occasionally, the reader was hypercritical, which damages an author too.

Whether you work with beta readers on the editing phase or not, prepare yourself for an emotional roller coaster. It will be challenging but it's worth it. The right editors can be your superheroes, saving the day for you and your book in this part of the publishing adventure.

THE EDITING ADDICTION—WHEN TO BREAK THE HABIT

You hire a content editor and the edits transform your manuscript from a melody to a song. Your next thought might be that if one round of editing made it so beautiful, perhaps a second round will make it an opera, right?

Wrong.

One of our clients hired her own editor after our editors were done following this thought. She thought the book would get 10x better again. Surprise! That editor found a bunch of things to change and some were in contradiction to what the other editors had suggested. She was furious with us because she felt our editors hadn't done their job.

The problem wasn't our editors, it was hiring more professionals and expecting the book will get better and better every time. Editors are hired to be opinionated. If you put your book through five different editors, they will have five different ways to improve your book. You will never leave the editing phase.

Not only that but your book will lose its focus and start getting worse instead of better. You're never going to have your book come back without any marks. And you shouldn't try.

Your book is NEVER going to be perfect. Make the book its best possible version and then put it into the world. A book that doesn't get published will never have an impact on your reader or your life.

BONUS TIP
AVOID DRAFT CONFUSION WHEN YOU WORK
WITH YOUR EDITORIAL TEAM

In our early days at Book Launchers, we had a client who wanted to work on her 80,000-word book every single weekend, her only free time.

The book was scheduled to go to an editor for three weeks, however. She insisted we split up the manuscript so she could work on one half while the editor worked on the other. We strongly recommended against this, but she was firm and a bit furious. We also weren't as experienced as we are now so we gave in.

We had some of the book in her hands, some in the hands of the editor, and much to our horror, she also sent part of the book to her writing coach for additional input.

During the second round of copy edits, we got a really angry and frustrated call from her because, somewhere along the way, a bunch of work she'd done on the book had disappeared.

It was nowhere to be found.

What happened was a bad case of "draft confusion." She didn't clearly label the manuscript so no one knew which one was the latest version. The one that ended up getting patched together had some changes but missed others.

She wound up having to take two weekends to redo it, and she was stressed the whole time about whether it was as good as the first time or if she was missing things.

The client blamed us, and it was ultimately our fault because we didn't follow our process. Today, we don't budge and adhere to strict document labeling conventions.

Waiting a week or two while an editor finishes work on your full manuscript will save you time and energy in the long run.

Now, draft confusion can happen even if you're not passing pieces of a book around like a hot potato. Here's how to prevent it from happening:

1. **Avoid the temptation to edit a book in pieces.** The first half of the book is not independent from the second half. Reading something in one area may trigger you or your editor to check and adjust something elsewhere. If pieces are missing, this can't happen, or notes have to be carefully made to try to do it next time you work on that piece.

2. **Update EVERY edit of your book with a new version number and the edit date** so that it looks like this: Book Title_Content_Edit_R1_Initials_Date.
   Each person who touches the book usually puts their initials on it, too, just to be clear. You're going to end up with a dozen different versions but you'll always be able to identify the most recent one. And if something gets deleted along the way that you want back, you can retrieve it from a previous version.

Writing a book is time consuming, so I understand the inclination to work on it whenever you have a clear moment. A better idea is to spend the time when your book is with the editor working on your author platform, connecting with influencers in your space, building a lead magnet, or heck, relaxing because there's much more work to come!

CHAPTER 10:

YOUR READER ONLY CARES ABOUT ONE PERSON, AND IT'S NOT YOU

"Look Mommy, there's a bear."

It was early one morning on a family vacation in Whistler, British Columbia. I had my two-year-old son, Jackson, in his stroller as we walked to the park.

"Oh, is there sweetie? Where?" I said, still not quite awake.

The words were barely out of my mouth when I saw a rather scruffy brown bear strolling right up to us on all fours! He (or she?) was about my height and had calm-looking brown eyes and a yellow tag in his left ear.

If I took two more steps, I could have reached out to pet him.

"Oh shit! There IS a bear!"

I turned the stroller around and ran toward a nearby store. I later realized I shouldn't have turned and ran. But seriously, come face-to-face with a bear while walking your toddler to the park and tell me what YOU would do!

Some people were inside the store, whose door was propped open, so I began yelling, "Bear! Bear!" Everyone looked at me calmly as if to say, "Oh, yeah?" But then they saw it. They sprang to action, ushering us in and locking the door behind us.

Seconds later, the bear sauntered up and circled the storefront a few times. He wasn't aggressive at all, just cruising around looking for food. But my adrenaline was off the charts.

After a few minutes, Jackson said, "That was scary!"

I don't think he was actually scared, but he knew I was.

Eventually, the bear wandered away and we went to the park, but my eyes stayed wide open for the rest of that trip.

Does this story help you write a better book? I hope that you were dying to find out what happened because that's the way a reader should feel when they pick up your nonfiction book. Your content shouldn't be boring, and it shouldn't be predictable.

That is the "bear" minimum you should go for.

Maybe so many nonfiction books are dull because they are written by highly educated people who have had their creativity beaten out of them.

By the time I graduated with my MBA, I was highly skilled at filling a page with words that ultimately said very little. Phrases like "think outside the box," "let's circle back on this," and (my personal favorite for ending a conversation) "at the end of the day." When I started writing for a major e-newsletter called "Early to Rise," my editor deleted those words from my work and eventually (mostly) from my mouth.

Higher education often teaches us how to focus on making ourselves sound intelligent so don't feel bad if you write with big words and jargon. That's what you've been taught. Now it's time to learn a new way—the way that leaves a reader wanting more!

One of our clients sent me the first draft of his book. About 80 percent of the chapters started with the word "I." As in, Chapter One: I experienced this. Chapter Three: I was in a meeting. And Chapter Four: I saw the trend.

Do you see the trend?

The author was writing his book about himself but not thinking about the most important person in the equation—his reader.

Your reader only cares about one person, and it's not you.

FOUR IDEAS TO START YOUR CHAPTER AND HOOK YOUR READER FROM BEGINNING TO END

1. **Start in the middle of the action.**

   Take a page from the movies or even TV shows. They throw you right into the middle of the action. The movie opens with the bombs going off, a chase scene, a shouting match, or some sort of heavy conflict or emotional turmoil.

   Maybe your book is about diet and fitness or investing for retirement. That's fine. You can still throw the reader into the middle of a story.

   Consider these opening lines:

   The message stood out on the bathroom wall, scribbled in bright red marker: "Whose is fatter than Alex? Fill in the blank below:

   ## *No One*

   You hear sobbing over the phone. "I have Stage 4 cancer," a feeble voice says.

The bank teller looked at me coldly and said, "Your account has $7.18 in it. Would you like it in dimes and pennies, or do you want me to find bills that small?"

Each sentence makes the reader at least curious enough to read the next line—especially if it's speaking to situations they've experienced in their own life.

2. **Start from an unusual point of view.**

   If you're writing a book about fighting cancer, why not start from the perspective of the cancer cell and what it wants?

   Maybe start from the perspective of the mutual fund company that charges a front-end loaded fee to exploit clients?

   Think about how things are typically explained and see if there is another way to do it.

   One of the Improv exercises I've seen done at The Groundlings was to tell a story from the perspective of being an odd item in a strange place. It's a fun exercise in expanding your story-telling skills. For example, telling the story as though you're a crumb stuck inside Sam Elliott's mustache. Or possibly a bookmark stuck inside a classic book.

   That's taking this to an extreme, but a little improv thinking will loosen you up to tell your story and present the material you have in an interesting and memorable way.

3. **Shock or surprise the reader.**

   Suspense is when the reader knows something is coming but they don't know what or when. Surprise is when you tell your reader something and it's totally unexpected. Like the time I was rushing out of my apartment, late for work, and realized I didn't have pants on. (True story, and I used it as the opener of my second book *The New Brand You.*)

Lies and scandals can be surprising. Facts and statistics can surprise too. Make sure you choose things that will make someone stop in their tracks.

I challenge you to open one or two chapters with something most people won't know. Surprise or shock them.

4. **Make it important.**

Hit readers hard with a statement or promise that this is the chapter that will make them rich. Happy. Faster. Fitter. Prettier. Smarter. More popular. More loved. More admired by their neighbors. Let them know that at the end of it, they'll be better off. That should keep them reading or entice them to buy the book if they're just browsing and happen to see that particular paragraph.

Your first chapter should have the most powerful opening line, but think about every chapter like the opportunity that it is: to get and keep your reader's attention.

While you're at it, take a look at the chapter title again. We touched on it before but is that chapter title compelling? Will it make someone curious? If it's not, brainstorm how you can make it better. Nobody needs another chapter called "Finding Your Why."

Remember, you're writing this book to have an impact on the reader. That only happens if they keep reading!

CHAPTER 11:

20 PAGES CAN MAKE OR BREAK YOUR SALE

Ever sniff a book? My friend Deb goes to bookstores, opens up books, and smells! Like the smell of a new puppy or a baby's head, there are people who love the smell of books. There is even a word for it, according to the Urban Dictionary: bibliosmia.[30]

Want your book to sell better on Amazon? Maybe you need to make it smell better! Ha! I'm just kidding. But did you notice how I started this chapter in an interesting way? I used a surprising fact. I have one more for you which I will share in a minute. But first, let's cover what really will help your book sell better on Amazon (and pretty much everywhere else too).

Take a look at the first 20 pages of your book and remove *everything* that doesn't sell your book. Period.

Always be thinking book marketing. When you're thinking book marketing, you're thinking about the reader of your book and the buyers of your books. How will you appeal to them? What will impact them the most?

---

30 "Bibliosmia," Urban Dictionary, accessed September 4, 2020, https://www. urbandictionary.com/define.php?term=bibliosmia.

EVERYTHING from the book title, book cover, book description, and first pages in a book matter far more than you can realize.

If your book cover, title, and description do a good job of getting your ideal reader's attention, they will look at the table of contents next. If they see a few chapters that make them feel like they need this book, they may buy it right there, or they may go to the next couple of pages. What's in those next few pages are vital. Let's take a look at what most authors do and what you will do so that you sell way more books than most authors.

THE "LOOK INSIDE" FEATURE ON AMAZON HAS CHANGED BOOK BUYING FOREVER

The "Look Inside" feature automatically turns on if you have a Kindle book on Amazon. It's flexible viewing limit can be set from 10–80 percent of the book. The default setting is 20 percent. If you have a 250-page book, the first 25 pages are what you need to focus on because that first 10 percent is what a reader will be able to see.

Look at every single page with a marketer's eye. Is this page compelling enough for a potential reader to buy my book? If they're reading it, are they going to keep reading?

With that in mind, let's go through the most common first pages, including your book dedication, foreword, acknowledgements, prologue, and anything else readers typically see before Chapter 1 in a book.

DOES YOUR BOOK DEDICATION SELL YOUR BOOK?

Fun fact for you: 80 percent of people read book dedications, according to research by Canadian author David Chilton.[31] In contrast, the study found more than half of readers skipped the introduction.[32]

You're probably not thinking about your reader when you write your dedication but you should be!

You may think this page is your own personal spot in the book to write whatever you want. But if you're a smart, marketing-savvy, reader-focused author—you will realize this is the first taste your readers get of you.

Have you made them curious? Do they feel even a tiny bit connected to you after they read it?

Here's my first dedication in *More than Cashflow* before I knew anything about book marketing:

> *To my Grandpa Broad, more than any property he ever owned or any business he ever ran, nothing was more important than his family.*

I didn't crush it, but it does set the tone for a book that is all about why you need to focus on the life you're trying to create rather than how to make more money as a real estate investor.

The dedication in Thomas Gabor's book, *Enough: Solving America's Gun Violence Crisis* reads:

> *To the victims of gun violence and their families, as well as the activists, researchers and healers working to alleviate the suffering from the scourge.*

---

31 David Chilton is the Canadian author of *The Wealthy Barber*, which sold more than three million copies. He went on to support many major authors, including the creators of the Loony Spoons Cookbook series.

32 "Up Your 'Dedication' Game," The Chilton Method, accessed September 4, 2020, https://booklaunchers.com/chilton.

That is a great dedication that also sets the tone for his book. It makes you FEEL the impact of the problem and how many people are trying to solve it.

Depending on your book topic and your personality, you could try to be humorous:

In Chilton's course on book marketing, he said one of his favorite dedications was by an author who wrote, "To my 2 fabulous wives – I pray you never meet."

Lanae St. John has a book called *Read Me: A Parental Primer for "The Talk."* She has a two-part dedication, but the second part is focused on her reader and shares what she hopes they take from her book:

> *To the generations that come after us—I wish all of you passionate healthy loving sex lives free of shame, guilt, and stress where you love and are loved deeply in all the ways YOU define it. Take care and love one another!*

The dedication is an opportunity to set the tone for your book. Please don't feel you need to dedicate it to your spouse and kids. And your dog can't read so you can leave your fur baby out of it. Once you write one book, you'll likely write others so you can save dedications up for future books.

Now, let's touch on Acknowledgments and Forewords.

ABOUT THAT BORING BOOK ACKNOWLEDGMENTS SECTION

Have you ever watched the Academy Awards?

Do you like it when your favorite actor gets up there and says,

I'd like to thank the Academy and Screen Actors Guild. I also would not be here if it weren't for Joe Agent, Alice Manager, Suzie Makeup, Mike Wardrobe, and the cast of the show, most notably, blah-blah-blah...

About 30 seconds later, the names are still pouring out, and you're grabbing snacks and drinks waiting for the good stuff.

That's 99 percent of acknowledgments.

Most readers only read the acknowledgments after they have read and loved a book. If that's the case, and most people find them incredibly dull, why put the acknowledgments at the front of their book?

EVERY DETAIL OF YOUR BOOK MATTERS WHEN IT COMES TO BOOK MARKETING

The most important information for book marketing purposes reside in the first 5–7 percent of your book. If you throw in two pages that resemble a dull Oscars acceptance speech, do you think you're doing a good job of selling your book? Unless there is a VERY strategic reason for including the acknowledgments at the front of your book—and I can't think of one right now—put them at the back.

Also, have fun with them.

The best Oscar winners tell a story. They make you laugh, they shout out a call to action, or they make you cry. But that's still rare because most are as boring as dry toast.

Bring a little personality to it. Imagine it's your Oscar speech and your one shot to tell the world what's really important. What do you want to say? Make it a challenge to come up with the most creative ways you can acknowledge the contributions of other people. This is how Rob Berger, author of *Retire Before Mom and Dad*, did it:

> *My wife, Victoria, has managed to survive this life with me by her side for nearly 31 years and counting. For that alone, she deserves a medal.*

You don't have to thank the academy or a publisher—because you're INDIE, BABY! But if you do want to thank Book Launchers, I'm totally cool with that.

THE COPYRIGHT PAGE IS MORE IMPORTANT THAN YOU THINK

The copyright page is important to librarians, publishers, bulk book buyers, bibliographers, and even writers who want to quote your book. This is an important page, even if it's not that exciting.

First, before we get into what is on the copyright page, you might be wondering what is copyright and what you need to do to protect your book?

There's good news, author. From the moment you put pen to paper (or your words to word processor), it's protected by copyright. Regardless of the media, if you live in North America, automatic copyright applies.

This can be confusing because if protection is automatic, then why would you want to file and pay money for an official copyright certificate?

If you've written a book and you have to defend your copyright in court, then you need your copyright certificate. The copyright page in your book does not qualify as a legal document. If registration occurs within five years of publication, it's considered *prima facie*, which loosely translates to "at first appearance." In nonlegal terms, that means it's accepted as true unless concretely proven otherwise.

Also, if you expect your book and audience to be international, it's worth noting that there are 20 countries in the world that require you to file a copyright because they don't recognize automatic copyrights.[33] Which means, in those countries, someone could republish

---

33 "What is Copyright?" RightsDirect, accessed September 4, 2020, https://www. rightsdirect.com/international-copyright-basics/.

your work and you have no defense in their courts unless you file for copyright.

The second reason to file for copyright is to have your book considered for inclusion in the Library of Congress.

It's not a necessary step to publish a book but it can be a wise step in your publishing process. If you file for copyright, there's very little that can be questioned about timeline and ownership in the future.

One important thing to understand is that copyright applies to your work, not your ideas. Ideas cannot be copyright protected.

The copyright page in your book typically includes:

- The copyright notice
- The edition information
- Publication information
- Printing history
- Cataloging data
- Legal notices
- ISBN or other identification numbers

Some books also contain credits for design and editing or illustration.

Some of that is optional. **The most important thing to have on the copyright page is, SURPRISE…the copyright!** It's the C symbol or the word copyright, which can be abbreviated cop or *C-O-P-R* followed by the year of first publication and the copyright owner.

The owner could be you, your company or, if you're going the traditional publishing route, it will be the publishing company to which you've assigned your rights. We'll talk about your publishing company in a moment.

Other things that you might want to include on the copyright page include your reservation of rights, which outlines what people can and can't do with your protected material. It typically reads as:

You may also include the publisher's contact information with an email address or a website. This can be really useful if someone wants to purchase books or ask you for permission to reprint more than a quote from your book. You can always put that information at the back of the book too.

You can also include trademark information if you've trademarked your book title, publishing company imprint, or if you're pursuing a Library of Congress listing.

A trademark is different than a copyright. Both are intellectual property but a trademark has more value. It must be registered and must be unique. There are different kinds of trademarks. **An ordinary trademark** includes words, designs, tastes, textures, moving images, mode of packaging, holograms, sounds, scents, three-dimensional shapes, colors, or a combination of these things. They will be used as a way to identify a company, product, or service.

A certification mark can be licensed to many people or companies for the purpose of showing that certain goods or services meet a defined standard.

You may choose to try to trademark your book title or your publishing company if it's part of a bigger business plan. But many words are not eligible for a trademark, so you'll need to hire an attorney to do a search and then register the trademark if it is eligible. If you do this, put the information of the trademark or pending trademark on your copyright page.

If you look at other books, you may notice a series of numbers on the copyright page. This indicates print runs but it's not really relevant in today's Print-On-Demand world. (A video explaining Print-On-Demand versus Offset is available at booklaunchers.com/notboring.)

This is only one page in your book so include only the elements that are the most important to you as it pertains to the publishing of your book.

THE GUIDE TO FOREWORDS

Phew—now that got a little technical—so let's take a moment to celebrate the value in books. Some books are worth millions centuries after their publication!

Leonardo da Vinci's *Codex of Leicester*, also known as the *Codex Hammer*, is currently the most expensive book ever sold. It's a 72-page book on linen. It's more of a journal than a book, as far as I can tell, and in 1994, Microsoft founder Bill Gates paid $30.8 million for it.[34]

If Leonardo da Vinci's notebook sold for millions, imagine if he wrote a foreword for your book? You might ask, how much is a celebrity foreword worth?

There's absolutely no reason to pay someone to write a foreword for your book. If you don't know anybody famous to write your foreword, your book is not doomed. Let me repeat, *your book is not doomed.*

What's a book foreword?

It's an introduction to your book and to you, the author. It's also written by someone other than you. If it's done right, by a person who is widely known in the circle of people you wish to impress, this can give you status and credibility.

---

34 Carol Vogel, "Leonardo Notebook Sells for $30.8 Million," *The New York Times*, November 12, 1994, https://www.nytimes.com/1994/11/12/us/leonardo-notebook-sells-for-30.8-million.html.

For example, if you've written a book on entrepreneurship and Sarah Blakely pens your foreword, or if you have a book on social media and Gary Vee gives you a foreword, or a book on environmental tech in business and Elon Musk endorses your work in a foreword, that will go a long way in establishing you as an expert and a voice that should be heard.

The most important thing to keep in mind is that this content, too, needs to sell your book. Here are some ideas:

- If the writer of the foreword has a cool story about you that will provide context for your book, it can give the reader interesting information they won't find elsewhere in the book.
- If the story or commentary in the foreword shines a positive light on your work and provides pertinent research that is interesting and relevant, the reader will benefit and see you in a positive light.
- If the writing is engaging or humorous, it provides the reader with even more of a reason to read the book.

If the foreword doesn't accomplish at least two of the above objectives, it really shouldn't be in the book, even if it's written by someone famous. Regardless, it should be fewer than 500 words, no matter who writes it!

Remember, the first 10 percent of your book is viewable online before it's purchased.

Because a foreword is deeply personal, it's tough to ask a complete stranger to write it. It's much better to approach him/her to endorse your book with a blurb. A foreword, on the other hand, is seen as a personal introduction, or endorsement. That's why it can be really powerful with the right person, but it's also why it's hard to get someone to do it unless you pay them or you have a long-standing relationship.

Does the person writing the foreword need to read the book?

If the book isn't done or the person who has agreed to endorse it is busy, they might not be able to read all of your book. Instead, their foreword will serve more as an introduction of you and your work to the reader. Hopefully, they can explain why you are unique and why your work matters, relating that back to the subject matter of your book. They can also write why readers will benefit from learning about you and your perspective on this subject.

USING QUOTES IN YOUR BOOK

What can you do with someone else's copyrighted work? When you write a nonfiction book, you are likely to quote other people's work. Or you may use other people's work as references. In many cases, you're interviewing other people.

What is considered "fair use" for you to put into your book and what requires citation or permission? And what is just outright not OK?

First, this is not legal advice. I hire a lot of lawyers in my business but I'm not a lawyer myself. If you need legal advice, please consult a professional with publishing expertise.

What you do need to know is that "fair use" is a US legal term that allows you to use *brief* excerpts of copyrighted material for purposes such as criticism (in other words, both good or bad reviews), new reporting, teaching, and research. In those cases, there's no need for permission from the creator or copyright holder.

The word that should be noted is *brief*.

There's no word limit but the amount of material used must be reasonable to serve its purpose. In other words, it's a judgment call. But unless there's a really clear argument as to why you need an entire section of a book or an entire speech or song, stick to the most important line or two and you'll be fine. No matter what, it's important to give the copyright holder or original author credit.

US copyright law doesn't require attribution, but how would you feel if someone quoted your work and didn't give you credit? That's pretty crappy.

For more on Fair Use, I highly recommend you check with the Fair Use Guide by the Author's Alliance.

FIVE UNCONVENTIONAL TIPS TO AVOID BORING BOOK INTRODUCTIONS

A quick Google search for "how to write a book introduction" lands you some advice like:

1. Summarize or outline the book.

2. Provide an overview of the book with your reader hook.

3. Share why you wrote the book.

4. Tell them who the ideal reader is and what the intended use or outcome is for the book.

Are you still awake? Probably not, because we've got a total snooze fest right there!

Even if you don't follow that advice, you've probably written an introduction that is incredibly author focused, and the reader isn't really that interested in learning all about you and why you wrote the book just yet. Remember, they are really only interested in what your story will do for them. You need to speak to that in your introduction.

Here are my five tips for writing a book-selling introduction:

1. **You might not need one at all.** If you're following our advice for creating awesome chapters, then your first chapter probably will knock a reader's socks off.

   Let's take an example from Rachel Hollis' book, *Girl, Stop Apologizing*. Her introduction starts, "When I originally started writing this book, I fully planned on calling it Sorry, Not Sorry. And, yes, I was basing that title on Demi Lovato's song." The introduction goes on page after page, and while well-written, it's really not about the reader or even for the reader. It's all about the author.

Rachel Hollis fans may love it, but if I didn't know that Rachel Hollis is a super-hot, best-selling author and this is a follow-up book to her popular *Girl, Wash Your Face*, I wouldn't keep reading.

Now, compare that to how Rachel Hollis starts her No. 1 *New York Times* best-selling book, *Girl, Wash Your Face*. The first chapter is titled "The Lie: Something Else Will Make Me Happy" and starts, "I peed my pants last week. Not full-on peed my pants, like that one time at summer camp when I was 10 years old."

That's how you start a book. It immediately sucks you into a story and makes you want to know more.

Your book doesn't need an introduction if you crush your first chapter and have a great book cover and description. But I get it. I'm a traditionalist too. I like a to-the-point, reader-focused intro.

So maybe this tip is for you:

2. **Go straight to the promise of the book.** Just tell them: "It sucks when you feel angry all the time. You get mad at your kids for asking for dinner. You yell at your dog for whining to go out to pee. And when you stub your toe, you burst like a volcano erupting. That's not a fun way to live. I know, I've been there. Once I got so mad, I yelled at a stop sign for telling me to stop. But you can get calm without going to anger management. You can find joy in little things. And you can do it with just a simple technique you're about to learn. In less than

seven minutes a day, this is going to help you. It helped me. It's helped John. You'll meet him soon."

For the record, I've never yelled at a stop sign. I just wanted to make up something that was concise and benefit driven. Tell the reader why they need to read this book. Don't assume the person reading the introduction has bought the book because often they have not. Even if they have, be bold and sell them on why they need to read it! Just like your book will never have an impact if you don't publish it, it also won't impact anyone who doesn't read it!

3. **Make sure your intro is all about the reader, even if you tell a story or talk about yourself.** See, in my fake intro that I just told you about yelling at a stop sign, that was a story about "me" for the purpose of relating to the reader. I wasn't rambling about a story about how I found enlightenment or got inspired or why I gave the book the title I did. I'm basically saying to the reader, "I understand you're angry and you don't like it. Here's how this book will help you."

4. **Keep it short.** Remember, this book is for your reader. It's intended to help them make a change, solve a problem, or achieve another important goal. Don't make them wait too long until you get to that.

And finally,

5. **Make sure there's a clear call to action to read the book right now.** A great intro covers the problem, offers the solution, and makes the reader realize they shouldn't wait. To make my fake intro better, I could tell the reader the cost of waiting. I could say, "Maybe you don't think you need to read this book today. But if you don't, you could be damaging your relationships beyond repair and you're certainly missing out on a lot of love and joy that you'll be open to once you know the tricks in this

book. So what are you waiting for? Calmer waters are ahead. Keep reading."

If your intro is too long or too boring or all about you, you may still get book sales but you'll never know the ones you miss out on. You also don't know how many people buy your book but never read it!

Start your book strong to get sales and sell the reader on actually reading your book. It's not just about having that new book smell... you need your book to sell too.

CHAPTER 12

SOMETIMES IT'S GOOD TO BE A CONTROL FREAK

"What the heck?" I thought as I read a new book on buying foreclosed properties in the US. The stories were familiar but it was recently published and I had never heard of the author.

How could I possibly know this material? I was so confused!

As I kept reading, that feeling of déjà vu would not go away. Then, near the end of the first chapter, I immediately recognized the source. I went to my shelf, grabbed a book written by a friend of mine, and I did a side-by-side comparison. Sure enough, it was the same book but a different title and author. Everything else was the same—including the publisher!

I was stunned. I figured my friend knew, but I wrote him anyway to ask what had happened. He let me know the publisher took his name off the book because he'd left the real estate industry and wasn't promoting his book anymore. He wasn't pleased, but the part that upset him the most was that he had two coauthors on the book who were still in real estate and they were removed from the book too.

The publisher took all of their stories and republished them under someone else's name without attributing the original authors. It was morally gross but legally legit, according to my friend's book contract.

When you work with a traditional publisher, they typically get the rights to your book and everything in it. You need to read the contract carefully and decide if it's really worth it to give up so much to get that book deal.

Frankly, since we're talking about rights and contracts, let's be clear: A lot of companies say they help you "self-publish" but then take rights or a ridiculous amount of your royalty on top of charging you fees. As we get into publishing decisions for your book, we'll clear up what makes sense for you, what's shady, and what's an outright scam.

SCAMS, SHADE, AND SENSIBLE CHOICES FOR SELF-PUBLISHERS

#1 Who owns the rights?

Ian Szabo wrote an excellent book called *From Renos to Riches*. A production company wanted to turn it into a TV show *but* his publisher wasn't cooperating.

The publisher owned the rights to the title and book concepts, which were vital to the potential show. Without the publisher's cooperation, he had to buy the rights back to his book to pursue the TV opportunity. He never disclosed what that cost but he had to buy every copy of his book in circulation.

Again, it's not a scam for a publisher to own the rights, that is part of the deal. But as a subject matter expert or someone with a powerful story, your number one priority should be to control as much of your intellectual property as you possibly can. If you give up any rights—including concept rights, international rights, audiobook rights, e-book rights, among others—make sure you receive ample compensation.

Also ask a lot of questions or consult a professional so you know exactly what you're getting into.

The more you can control, the bigger the potential for profit and opportunity if your book becomes really popular.

When you work with someone else to produce your book, make sure they give you all the related files and that any contracts explicitly state this. We've had so many authors come to Book Launchers when a company has gone out of business or has done a poor job on their book and they don't have source files. We have to recreate the book again in order to make changes and publish the book. Even if you own the rights, make sure you've got all the word documents, InDesign files, e-pubs, jpegs, charts, and graphs.

Even if you don't have the software to edit these materials, still be sure to get the files so you or someone else can make changes to your book in the future and use it however you want. If a company won't give you this contract provision, it's a huge red flag.

#2 How are guarantees fulfilled?

If anybody guarantees you'll win an award or become a bestseller, ask specifically how they intend to make it happen.

Most of our authors receive a new release Amazon Best Seller ribbon, but in many cases, they get that ribbon after selling as few as 25 copies of their book. It's not that hard to get. Some companies charge $5,000 to get you that ribbon because the average new author doesn't realize how easy it is to earn. That's why it's important to clarify how any guarantee is fulfilled.

If you're an "award-winning author" but every single author who works with their company gets an award, how legit is that? If your future clients or partners find out your award was basically a paid participation award, will that really do positive things for your credibility and brand?

Oh, and if you're still hung up on that Amazon Best Seller ribbon, chew on this fact for a second: When you get that ribbon, you won't be able to advertise it. Even Amazon doesn't consider it legitimate and will remove any mention of it from your account. In fact, when you are no longer on the list, you have absolutely nothing to show for it except your screenshot.

#3 Who gets the royalties?

Amazon opened the door for independent publishing but also put some serious downward pressure on book prices. This means there are less profits to go around, so why wouldn't you want to receive 100 percent of any profits from every book sold?

Even if you're fine with giving up some of your hard-earned royalties in exchange for something else from a company, such as bookstore distribution or a reduced cost of production upfront, make sure you know who's getting the royalties and how much is really being spread around.

#4 Who owns the ISBN?

The ISBN, which stands for International Standard Book Number, is a publisher identifier. Many companies say, "We'll assign you an ISBN" and they sell it like a benefit. Or they'll say, "You don't need to worry about bringing it, we'll give you one." But if you want to own the rights to your book and fully control it now and forever, come to the table with your own.

If you're in Canada, you can get an ISBN for free through the Library and Archives Canada website. In the US, you have to buy one. You can get an individual ISBN for $125 through Bowker (https://www.myidentifiers.com), the official website of the US ISBN agency, or buy a pack of 10 for a little more. Since you need a different ISBN for each format of your book and they never expire, I'd splurge for the 10 pack.

#5 How do you get copies of your book?

Some companies charge you $2 per copy of the book PLUS printing costs to get copies of your own book! Many of our authors are speakers and sell thousands of books directly to companies and organizations that hire them to give talks. Every time they do that, their publisher is making thousands of dollars for doing nothing but putting in an order and setting up shipping.

With Print-On-Demand, you have absolutely no reason to ever do a deal like this. Set up your own accounts and order directly from Ingram. If you want to set up some bulk book arrangements, there are some great companies that will ship them for your speaking engagements and take a much smaller cut from your profits than $2 a book.

You're doing the hard work of producing an excellent book and then using it to land these gigs and deliver the talks, make the most money you can from every book sold!

AMAZON ASIN VS. ISBN

Amazon gives you a book identifying number for free if you use their KDP print service, so you might be wondering if it's worth buying your own ISBN.

The ASIN, the Amazon Standard Identification Number, is a unique block of 10 letters and numbers that identify items. You can find the ASIN on Amazon's product information page. An ISBN is the acronym for International Standard Book Number. This 10- or 13-digit number identifies a specific book, an edition of a book, or book-like product such as an audiobook.

If you have an ISBN number, then the ASIN can be the same number. But if you don't have an ISBN, Amazon assigns you an identifying number for use only on Amazon.

Are you confused yet?

Here's what you really need to understand in this whole mess of letters and numbers:

If you want to sell your book anywhere other than Amazon, you should get your own ISBN.

You need one for each version of your book sold outside of Amazon, including e-book, softcover, hardcover, audio, and large print.

If you want bookstores, libraries, Apple, or listings with Kobo or Google Play, you need your own ISBN.

A free ASIN won't let you be listed as publisher. Amazon is listed as the publisher and to many people, it can make you look just a little less professional.

Whatever you choose to do, it is important to know that you will still own the copyright to your book. Ownership is yours. You just limit the reach of your book.

Don't Get Ripped Off by Bowker or Anyone Else: Here's a little bonus tip when you are buying your ISBN—do not buy anything but the ISBN from Bowker. (Bowker is the only authorized distributor of ISBNs in the US. Every country has only one legal source for ISBNs so check your country's source.) You don't need to pay for a barcode. You can create barcodes using free tools on the internet, KDP Print upload will do it, or your book cover designer can do it. Just buy your ISBN.

ARE AWARDS WORTH IT FOR AUTHORS?

I know someone who paid $20,000 to become an award-winning author. She had a celebrity coauthor, wrote one chapter, and when the book launched, she flew to a city for a swanky red carpet event to receive an Oscar-style award. They had professional photographers take pictures and she posted them everywhere. Boom! She's now an award-winning author.

I asked her if she thought it was worth it. "I think it helped with my credibility," she replied.

If people knew the award was given to her because she paid for it, I'm certain it would be the opposite.

But I get it. Authors everywhere are hungry for exposure, validation, and credibility so the author award business is huge. And here's my confession: I was one of those authors! I paid to enter my books into a lot of competitions. My first book, *More Than Cashflow*, won an international book award. My second, *The New Brand You*, won the Beverly Hills Book Award for Best Sales Book and a couple other accolades. These weren't as hokey as paying someone to give you awards but they were part of for-profit businesses, which is a little bit sketchy.

The fee to enter makes sense because there are processing fees but if there is no monetary prize, where does all the money go? You might think it goes toward judging but as I researched these kinds of prizes, I found very few actually disclose the identity of the judges. It makes me wonder, does anybody even read these books? In some cases, it's likely nobody does. You don't get feedback and there isn't anything written about the winning books to indicate why they were selected. Almost none of these questionable awards will tell you how many books were in your category so you could be a winner in a category of one. Many have hundreds of categories because they want to encourage everyone to enter. Some sell merchandise if you win and require you to buy proof of your award—a sticker or a plaque—if you want to share it.

A few places have what I would call a non-prize "award," including a press release, media announcement, even database and website listings are considered prizes. Others offer little more than the supposed honor of winning the award, which is truthfully all I got in the Beverly Hills contest.

Now that I know this, will I be submitting my next book to award companies? Only if:

- It's an award that honors authors and is doing it for the good of the community.
- They share a list of judges who give specific feedback.
- There's a tangible prize, like money that shows they are really trying to support the work of authors, not just make a profit.

(For a current list of credible awards to which we submit authors, you can visit: booklaunchers.com/notboring.)

Mostly, I recommend your focusing on finding people to read your book. Save those entry fees for thank you gifts for those who go over and above to support you in your ventures.

And remember, intellectual property is your greatest asset so evaluate every publishing contract with that in mind.

CHAPTER 13:

YOUR COVER IS CLICK BAIT AND YOUR DESCRIPTION SELLS

"We recommend you wear a navy blue suit for the first interview and a brown suit for the second interview. This conveys professionalism, confidence, and intelligence."

Ahh, business school, where we're taught to look like the perfect corporate employees. The fundamental message: **be like everyone else and you'll get a high paying job.**

If your goal is a six-figure salary, the advice works. If your goal is selling books, being like everyone else does the opposite—it makes it hard to get noticed. At the same time, there's a fine art to standing out while also being accepted and trusted. If you show up in an unexpected or radical way, people may not trust your message. Getting noticed is an art you must master for your book to succeed.

DO-IT-YOURSELFERS AND TEMPLATES NEED NOT APPLY – COVER DESIGN

You need to get the title right, but once you have that, your book cover is your next most important marketing tool. Getting it right is worth investing time and money on a professional to do it.

We've hired all kinds of graphic designers to create book covers over the years. We even hired a couple of folks who designed album covers and magazine covers. They had more than a decade of design experience and a ton of talent but without specific book cover designing experience, we struggled and had to spend a lot of time training them on the nuances of cover design.

We had a client who hired her book cover designer from Upwork. The cover looked good but when we went to upload it, there were issues with the bleed, spine size, and the font. We needed the source file to make adjustments, but the client hadn't been given the source file and couldn't track down the original designer after they left Upwork. We had to redesign the cover to get it right.

Another client hired a designer through 99Designs but the covers looked like templates. We ended up hiring our cover designer to direct the client's designer, and we still needed to make a bunch of changes to make an original standout cover.

The best way to find a great cover designer is to get a referral and then look at their book cover portfolio. Make sure they've done covers in your space and that you like their work. You'll need to be prepared to manage the process to get exactly what you want.

What is this going to cost? Reedsy, an author service firm based in London, outlines the average cost of covers for self-published authors. They said a relatively new book designer charges between $300 and $500. Experienced designers charge between $500 and

$800. And top tier, award-winning cover designers charge between $800 and $1500.[35]

You can always start on a budget and change the cover later if your book doesn't sell, but you'll never know the sales you lost by not nailing that cover in the first place.

If you want to see a great example of the difference in cover quality you get at each price-tier, check out the video by Self-Publishing with Dale where he hired five different cover designers at different rates to design the same cover. It's an excellent illustration of the difference between $50 and $800 cover designs (and everything in between). Visit booklaunchers.com/notboring for this link.[36]

To get best results with a designer:

1. Know the general category and genre of your book before designing the cover. We use the software tools by Publisher Rocket and KDSPY to help us research book categories for our clients. You can also do it manually on Amazon by looking at your competition and checking their category.

   You need to get familiar with other books in your category be-cause your book has to have similar characteristics. This is not the same as looking like them but fitting in. For example, when you look at celebrity memoirs, the author is almost always on the cover. Compare that to self-help, where the author is never on the cover, which tends to be simple and more neutral in color.

2. Choose a color palette. If you have brand colors in mind, that's great, or perhaps you have some colors that mean something to you or you know will stand out. Michael Brenner, author of *Mean People Suck*, knew a lime green cover was going to stand out and become part of the branding around his book. It sure

---

35 For more information: https://blog.reedsy.com/book-cover-design/
36 https://youtu.be/7__-AhQE4WY

did and all of his marketing popped. Narrowing your color choices will help make the designer's job a lot easier.

3. Find 5–10 covers you like and be able to tell the designer why you like those covers. They don't have to be covers from your category but you do need to be able to say what elements drew you in. Was it the picture, the simplicity, the font on the title, the colors, or some other piece of that cover that made you put it at the top of your list? Take a little bit of time to think about this before you hire a designer and you're more likely to get a design that feels like your book.

4. Know your cover dimensions and formats—or at least have a sense of what you think you want. This is called "trim size," and it's the publishing term for book size. After each copy is printed and bound, the book is mechanically trimmed so the size of every page is uniform. Typical nonfiction books are 6 x 9. But there are other formats, of course. More information about book size is available at: booklaunchers.com/notboring.

   This is important: When you hire your book cover designer, request covers for softcover, e-book, 3D, and hardcover versions (specify a dust jacket or case laminate), which all have distinct specifications. If you know you're doing an audiobook, ask for that too. Your audiobook cover is a totally different size than the other covers so you need a different design!

   Also, always ask for the original source files because you may want to make changes in the future or you might encounter issues when you upload and need to get the files revised. Always control your content. You own it. Don't worry about the fact that you probably can't open the files on your computer without the right software—just get the source files!

5. All of your cover matter must be supplied to the designer, including the book title, the subtitle, and your name (or any oth-

er name). Provide your publishing company logo if you created one. (For the inside flaps and back cover, you'll also need your book description, author bio, author photo, blurbs, ISBN, and any other specific images you want included.)

Here's a Quick Front Cover Checklist:

- Can you read the title (and ideally, the subtitle) in thumbnail size?
- Do the important words—the words that will matter to your ideal reader—stand out on the cover?
- Does the cover design fit with the genre, while still having something that makes it stand out? Photoshop it into a collage of the Top 20 book covers in your category to see.

DO YOU HAVE THE RIGHTS TO USE THAT IMAGE ON YOUR COVER?

When sourcing the images you may want on your cover, make sure you have the rights to use that image.

William Hung, the singer from *American Idol* who went viral, had tons of cool images of him on stage with Ricky Martin and other celebrities, but we couldn't use any of them on his cover. Just because it was his image didn't mean he owned the rights to use the photograph. In fact, buying the image for its use on a book cover was cost prohibitive. He ended up getting a professional photographer to take his picture and we used that on his cover.

Another cover situation involved a book about the Los Angeles fires of 2018. The cover designer found an incredible photo from Getty Images for the cover. We loved it and so did our client but the image was going to cost $1,500 to license for only three years.

That was a steep price to pay so Jaqueline Kyle, our book Production Manager, contacted the photographer directly and asked if he had any other similar photos available. He did and we were able to negotiate a much friendlier contract and a substantially lower cost.

The cover is stunning, and it was a great solution to an expensive problem.

BABY GOT BACK COVER TOO

Sure, you're probably going to sell more books online than in stores or in person but your back cover is still an important part of your book marketing. People see the front and back cover in online images. When your book is sitting on other people's shelves, on tables at conferences, or when it's being sold anywhere as a physical product, the back cover is the sales page. The title and the cover are the headline that grab attention but the other elements sell it. What do you put on the back cover to help it sell? Here are some tips:

1. **Treat it like it's a sales page.** The whole objective of the back cover of your book is singular: To sell your book. Your ideal reader needs to get so excited to read your book that they buy it, on the spot. Make sure that every word and image sells your book. Hire a copywriter if you need to—it's worth it.

2. **Skip the author photo.** Consider space carefully before putting your picture on the back cover. Great endorsements of your book are more valuable than your bio in many cases. If you have room, include a small image beside a concise bio. To save space or if there isn't enough value in your photo and bio taking up space on the back cover, put your photo and bio on the inside back flap or last page.

3. **Brilliant testimonials and endorsements.** If you can get three excellent testimonials for your book, they should go on the back cover. Each of them needs to have a compelling message to sell your book. Make sure they pack a punch by making

an appealing promise of what's inside or establishing your credibility.

4. **Put your website in the bottom left hand corner of your back cover.** People who don't buy your book might still go to your website and get your free download. Also, this is where people can go to learn more about you. It helps to establish your credibility and convince them that they need to read what you've written.

5. **Get a logo and a barcode.** To set up your publishing company and include it on the back cover and spine with a logo. The logo doesn't need to be fancy but including it on your book makes your book look that much more professional. If you aren't sure how to set up your publishing company we have videos that walk you through exactly what you need to know. You can view those at booklaunchers.com/notboring

Remember, the back cover has one job and that is to sell your book. If there is anything on it that doesn't make somebody rush to a cashier or click a "Buy" button, then you need to make some adjustments.

#noboringbook DESCRIPTIONS

Book descriptions are critical to selling your book and making those Amazon ads convert to sales. A book description, however, is not a summary of your entire book. It's a sales tool with a pitch and one job: to make the ideal reader *need* to read the book.

The opening sentence of that book description must grab their attention immediately. The first word has to be compelling. And the description should not be about the book, or about YOU. It's should be about what you are going to do for your reader.

Show the reader what's in the book for them. Here's where knowing the hook of your book will really help. What is the biggest promise of your book? Open with that.

Let me give you a few examples of book descriptions—three I like and one I do not.

This one is from the memoir *Educated* by Tara Westover: "Born to survivalists in the mountains of Idaho, Tara Westover was seventeen the first time she set foot in a classroom."[37]

This makes me curious.

Here's another description from *Read Me* by Lanae St. John: "Talking to your kids about sex is hard. And, oh so awkward."[38]

It grabs my attention and sets up with the problem she's going to solve.

Enough: Solving America's Gun Violence Crisis by author Thomas Gabor opens with this: "Life in America feels more dangerous today. There are 40,000 gun-related deaths each year and nearly *one mass shooting every day* in the United States."[39]

That gives me shivers and makes me stop. I want to read more, and if a reader wants to be part of the gun violence solution, they're going to buy this book.

Now here's one from *This is Marketing*, by Seth Godin, that I really think misses the mark of a good book description.

"Seth Godin has taught and inspired millions of entrepreneurs, marketers, leaders, and fans from all walks of life, via his blog, online courses, lectures, and best-selling books."[40]

---

37 Tara Westover, *Educated: A Memoir, Penguin Random House*, accessed September 4, 2020, https://www.penguinrandomhouse.com/books/550168/educated-by-tara-westover/.

38 Lanae St. John, *Read Me: A Parental Primer*, Barnes & Noble, accessed September 4, 2020, https://www.barnesandnoble.com/w/read-me-lanae-st-john/1131778878.

39 Thomas Gabor, *Enough! Solving America's Gun Violence Crisis*, Book Launchers, accessed September 4, 2020, https://booklaunchers.com/portfolio-item/enough-solving-americas-gun-violence-crisis/.

40 Seth Godin, *This Is Marketing: You Can't Be Seen Until You Learn to See*, Amazon, accessed September 4, 2020, https://www.amazon.com/This-Marketing-Cant-Until-Learn/dp/0525540830.

That is 100 percent about Seth Godin and while he's an awesome creator and entrepreneur, that's a terrible way to start a book description because it has absolutely nothing to do with the reader, especially one who is not familiar with Godin's work.

Make sure your book description is selling your book:

- ✔ Kick it off with an anecdote that highlights emotion or pain related to the problem you will solve. Use tension or curiosity if it's a memoir.
- ✔ Tease readers with what's inside the book that they haven't read before. Be specific. Most readers have already read at least one book like yours, so you must showcase specifics that make your book unique or hook them with your cool story.
- ✔ Show how their life is going to be different when the book is over or what they will experience that they're not getting from other forms of entertainment.
- ✔ Highlight the best tips, tools, or secrets in this book. A cool acronym or steps to solve a common problem in an uncommon way are great things to tease in the description. Ideally, these are little tidbits that should go in bullet points.
- ✔ Include a sentence or two about yourself and why you are the one person who can teach you. Make it personal. Remember the reader needs to look forward to spending hours with you as they read your book—make them excited to do that.
- ✔ Finally, use keywords. A great book description also includes the keywords that readers are likely to use to search for your book. If you're planning on running Amazon ads that will convert, this is extra important because you'll struggle to get your ads shown for specific keywords if you are not hitting the mark with them in your book description. The keywords you should focus on aren't ob-

vious, so we recommend you look at tools like PublisherRocket.com and KDSPY to figure this out. At Book Launchers, we also do Google Keyword research. We've found that a good keyword phrase in a book description can also result in your book being discovered more easily by search engines beyond Amazon.

✔ Be concise. For the description on the back cover, you're shooting for 120–160 words. Amazon and Goodreads have 4,000-character space limits but we typically go between 250–300 words to be sure it's not too long to grab someone's attention.

YOU ARE WHAT OTHER PEOPLE SAY, SO GET GOOD PEOPLE TO SAY COOL THINGS

Getting people to endorse your book is smart marketing. The absolute best endorsement is like Deepak Chopra's quote on the front cover of Alka Dhillon's book, *The OM Factor*:

"Alka eloquently shares how to bring spirituality in the business world by giving the tools and steps to the soul of leadership." **—Deepak Chopra, MD**, author of *The Future of God*

Nice work, Alka!!

Or this for the cover of Robert Kerbeck's book, *Malibu Burning:*

"Thrilling, well-researched, and occasionally lighthearted, *Malibu Burning* is a unique and special book." – Paul Kolsby, writer for the critically acclaimed Netflix series *Ozark*

Only the absolute best testimonials, also known as blurbs, should be considered for your coveted book cover space. The rest can go on Amazon, inside your book, and on media materials.

Ideally, you will collect testimonials that speak to three different aspects of your book, with the caveat that **anything that goes on your cover or in the book description needs to SELL your book.**

If any isn't cover worthy, you can still use them on your Amazon page, Author Website, or even put a collection of them inside your book if you'd like. Here are the three kinds that will help you the most with selling books:

1. **You are the person to write this book—the ONLY person**

   What makes you unique? What have you done? What's the most important piece of your story that differentiates you from other authors in your space?

   This is the first testimonial or endorsement you need to get. It could be something like this made-up example:

   "When I worked with Joe at Google, he was always the one to suggest the most creative and original solutions to problems so when he talks about creative thinking, I listen." – Joe Smith, VP, Google Product Development

   Shelley Buck and Kathy Curtis had some amazing endorsements for their book, *Leave Your Light On.*

   Check out this beautiful endorsement of Shelley:

   > *No matter when you encounter Shelley Buck, it is impossible not to be somehow transformed. Her raw willingness to trust, share, and guide is all evidenced in this new memoir, where she recounts the unforgettable journey of love, struggle, loss, and discovery, led by her son, Ryder.*

   Thomas Schumacher
   Producer of the Tony Award Winning Musical,
   The Lion King
   President Walt Disney Theatrical Productions

2. **How your book will benefit readers**

What's the reader going to take away from reading your book? And bonus points if the testimonial addresses any potential reader objections ("I know this already." "I don't have the time or money to do this.")

Ideally, a testimonial echoes your hook—the answer to WHAT'S IN IT FOR THE READER?

Along those lines, Gautam Baid's book, *The Joys of Compounding*, has a great testimonial:

"An instant classic! Gautam's book is the definitive guide to lifelong learning for investors and anyone seeking to reach their full potential. A must read." – Joh Mihaljevic, CFA, Chairman, MOI Global

This one gets bonus points because it spells out exactly who can benefit!

3. **This is worth the reader's time and curiosity**

    This kind of testimonial is best coming from a celebrity or popular author. If you don't know anyone like that, try a blurb from someone else that will make potential readers intensely curious.

    Rob Berger, the author of *Retire Before Mom and Dad*, got some heavyweights in the financial planning industry to endorse his book. If you are interested in personal finance, you'll know them. Consider this cool endorsement:

    "Clear, accurate, insightful. This might be the best introduction to financial freedom I've ever found." **-J.D. Roth author and founder of Get Rich Slowly**

    You're probably thinking, I don't know any celebrities. First of all, other than Deepak Chopra, I don't think any of these folks I've mentioned on these authors' books are truly famous but they're respected in their fields and that gives them credibility, which spills over to the authors.

The fact is, you don't have to know famous people; you just need a good strategy for contacting a bunch of people who are respected and known. And you need to do it with plenty of time to spare before your launch. Reach out to more people than you think you will need or think you can get. In other words, don't put all your eggs in one basket because often it's the one you least expect who will come through for you.

Here's how to get some great testimonials and endorsements for your book:

1. **Make a list of everyone you know.** Think about your friends, mentors, and clients who could write endorsements. Ideally, you're looking for people who can either speak to your expertise, offer their own credibility on your behalf, or provide a testimonial that speaks to what readers will gain from reading your book.

2. **Contact them.** Before you shoot out a mass email, remember each email needs to be personalized. Let them know why you think that they are the right people to provide a testimonial. A little flattery and genuine compliments go a long way. Try to build some rapport. Share quickly what your book is about and how you're publishing and marketing it. It takes time to write a good blurb, and they will feel better knowing the book could have reach and impact.

3. **Ask them how they would prefer to read your book.** Would they like a hard copy or a PDF? Let them know either format is easy to arrange.

4. **Follow up.** If you haven't heard back about your request, you can follow up once by email, or a maximum of two times, which could include a phone call. Don't be a pain. Just say,

"Hey, listen, I know you're busy and I'd just appreciate knowing if and when you can do this." If they've already agreed to provide blurb, promptly send them the manuscript and let them know your timeline. Be sure to give people enough time but not months and months. Tell them you'd love to consider their endorsement for the cover or inside flap of your book so you need it by a specific date.

5. **Collect the endorsements** and figure out which ones are going to be the best for your book cover, if any. Remember the three main types you need, and if they aren't amazing, they shouldn't go on the cover. If you have a lot of them, they can always go inside your book.

6. **File the endorsements** in a place where you'll have easy access to them when it comes time to begin marketing.

7. **Finally, express your gratitude.** Whether you use that blurb on the cover or not, send a thank you note. You can also send a signed copy of the book when it's published. They were willing to take their time and associate their name with your finished product, and that's pretty cool.

The most important advice I can offer here is to ask far more people than you think you will need—and start asking early. The most famous or notable folks are going to need the longest lead time. This is also another benefit of finishing your book early. Sure, you can send folks what is called an ARC (advanced reader copy) of your book but if they are going to endorse you, you want them to see the best possible version. That version is as close to final as possible.

SELFIES AREN'T GOOD ENOUGH — YOUR AUTHOR PHOTO

Whether it's going on the cover or not, you need a great author photo. It's time to update your headshot, so put on a nice shirt, get a haircut, and strike a writerly pose. Your author photo will be on your Amazon Author Page and on your book flap, PR Kit, podcast or Speakers One Sheet, Goodreads page, posters for your book signing, podcast interview show notes, and more.

How do you get your best shot?

First, hire a professional. This photo is going to be used over and over. It's worth the investment. When you're contracting the photographer, make sure they are going to give you at least three different edited shots with several changes of clothes and ideally, a few different settings and backgrounds. Some photographers will actually give you all your digital images but allow you to choose three to five to be edited. That's what you want so you have options and can get a consistent look for your brand and book.

You also want to ask your photographer to provide you with photographs in different sizes and a range of resolutions. For example, your Goodreads author profile needs to be a 400 x 400 pixel square. Many social media accounts will require a close-cropped square of your face, and you'll need other options for posters or other book-related promotional materials. Here's the list I would be giving a photographer:

- Waist-up shots (2–3) on a white background, resized four times to crop closer and closer to the face. One crop in a 400 x 400 pixel square. Be sure to specify at least one headshot.
- Personality (fun) shots (1–5) for use on book promotions and social media, resized for the web as well as print use.

The quantity varies, depending on the cost and your needs, but I like to have a variety because I don't do professional photo shoots very often! In fact, media often won't even do their own shots, they will ask for some of yours to choose from—so you will find having a variety is very useful!

Also, consider your background. I recommend white as it can be easily cropped out and also works for a variety of things. The author photo or headshot needs to be closely cropped. If you want social media shots though, backgrounds can add texture to the image. If the context of your book involves a specific setting, you could have a shoot where the images align with that context. For example, if you are writing about boating, it makes sense to have some shots near water. Or if your book is about your upbringing in small town USA, then some rural setting shots would work well.

Most importantly, find an outfit and a look that matches you and your brand and doesn't clash or blend in too much with the background. Stripes and bold patterns are generally too busy for small photos, so I recommend sticking with solid colors and several wardrobe changes.

Finally, if you tend to look stiff in photos, have a friend join you and chat with them during the shoot. You'll be more comfortable. The photographer may ask you for poses but your smile and eyes will be warmer if you're in the middle of a conversation with someone familiar.

Make your cover clickable and your description sell. It's a recipe for success when you already have the hook as your main ingredient. People really do judge a book by its cover, and you want yours to be judged favorably.

CHAPTER 14:

BEAUTIFUL FROM THE INSIDE OUT

Have you ever walked out of a movie because the sound was bad? Or there were issues with the picture? Or maybe you just hated the way the movie was shot so you stopped watching. The same kinds of things cause readers to put down a book.

Even worse, when it comes to a book, your reader will judge YOU based on the reading experience. There's nothing worse than putting your heart, soul, and money into a book, only to have people discount its value because it looks (gasp!) self-published!

One of the most common questions I get asked on podcasts, panels, and webinars is, "How can an author be sure their self-published book will sell?" Well, I can never guarantee anything, but if you treat your book like a hobby project, it might look like it was done on a budget and not appear as worthy as a traditionally published book. If you want to be seen as the expert, then you also need to invest in a great reading experience!

That experience isn't limited to the words on the page. It carries through to how those words are presented in the layout and design. If you're not paying attention as an author to all the details that impact your reader, you risk undermining all your hard work.

Whether that reader is a car salesman or the producer of *Good Morning America* evaluating whether to put you on their show, your book will be judged by more than its cover.

The cover of the book and it's interior—in print and digital—need to be polished. Editing isn't enough. The layout of the book needs to create a product that the reader enjoys holding in their hands and following with their eyes.

Few authors appreciate the intricate process of interior book design.

These days many free and low-cost conversion tools will take your Word document and turn it into a file that can be produced or published on Kindle or KDP Print. The ease and accessibility of these tools makes it seem like this is a straightforward process. The reality is that you can create something that will work but it's often noticeably not quite right. The best-case scenario is that a reader may not be able to put their finger on what is off but they will know it's off. The worst-case scenario is that major issues impact the experience so much they stop reading and give your book a bad review.

It's important for you to understand the basics of the process, and if looking like an expert is important, hire a professional layout person to design the interior of your book.

TYPESETTING WAS LITERALLY SETTING THE TYPE!

Have you heard of typesetting? Don't worry if you haven't. It's so nineteenth century, a time when people used to literally position physical letters onto pages for books to be printed. These were letter presses, and the words were set into place one letter at a time and then locked down.

The process jumped forward with the invention of hot metal typesetting, which used a keyboard like the typewriter, allowing someone to type out the desired text to be set.

These days, layout is accomplished with software but it's still a truly specialized skill. Most books need to be laid out, line by line, to be done right.

Here's a list of things your professional designer will guide you through:

- Size of the margins
- Trim size of the book
- Styling at the start of the chapters
- Images and graph insertion
- Font typeface and size
- Spaces between letters and lines

Our book designers use the cover of the book to establish style choices so we don't do interior until the cover has been complete. That way, the feelings evoked by the cover carry through and create a consistent experience for the reader.

If you choose to DIY your interior, you might choose a template because it seems easy. But while using a template may give you a starting point, you'll still have to correct each page manually line by line.

This is why it's one-part art and one-part science. Designers actually have to make grammar choices and style choices when they design a book, and it's extremely time consuming. If you want to do this yourself, I'm told that it's better to use a typesetting software like Vellum, which you can find at https://vellum.pub.

Details are not my strength nor are they remotely enjoyable so I would never be a happy DIY candidate for this. However, it's an option and eagle-eyed folks can get good results.

HIRING THE RIGHT INTERIOR DESIGNER FOR YOUR BOOK

Here are five tips for outsourcing a design worthy of your masterpiece manuscript:

#1 Ask about font packages

If you're working with an experienced book designer, they usually have a default font they use for nonfiction books. If they don't, they aren't experienced enough.

When you ask about their font package, all you really need to know is that a full package means it has italics, bold, and italic bold, plus full punctuation and symbols like the copyright and em dashes. A lot of font packages don't have the full selection, and you don't want to get halfway through a project and realize you don't have what you need. If that happens, you have to go back and choose a different package and do it over or adjust your book so it doesn't need a full package. Generally, for nonfiction, there are some common packages in Adobe like Adobe Garamond or Garamond.

#2 Take care of your orphans and your widows

If you're doing your book yourself, then you need to make sure you're going line by line and checking page by page so you aren't ruining a reader's flow with weird line breaks in the print book.

Breaking a paragraph in the wrong place can interrupt a reader's mental flow.

Widows occur when the last line of a paragraph ends up at the top of the next page, and an orphan occurs when the first line of a paragraph ends up at the bottom of the page.

You should look out for these errors when you review a print proof, but an experienced designer should also be trying to create a design that avoids them.

#3 Negative space is your friend

"Negative space" is the technical term for white space. White space in the form of large enough margins is important to maintain so someone can hold your book in their hands without covering up any words. There also needs to be space for the binding, and you don't want the text to be so squished that you can't read it.

There are also practical considerations like space for page numbers at the top and the bottom of the page.

Ultimately, it's about creating a design that is neither too busy and overwhelming or too spare and vacant.

#4 Elegance in simplicity

Don't go crazy and use every font and style available to you. Our designs often have the first letter of a chapter start with the same font from the cover or sometimes there are features from the subhead or other imagery that we use inside the book. These are subtle design touches, called "flares," that can enhance the experience. Focus on fonts that are comfortable for the eye to read the majority of the text in your book and then only use the flares on a limited basis to bring interest to each page.

#5 E-book conversion is a different game

Many authors get a great looking print design and then convert to an .ePub or .mobi file and everything becomes a mess. When we hire designers, we look at their interior file examples and then use e-book conversions as a final screening test. We've found that experienced designers set themselves up for successful e-book conversion and inexperienced ones don't. This is also why we really loathe Google Docs, which has to be stripped of all formatting before we go to design. Microsoft Word, in contrast, is a lot more publishing process-friendly.

It's also worth noting again that you need a book layout person who is an interior designer as much as a grammatical expert. It's a line-by-line job filled with choices to make sure the words are split correctly, lines end at the appropriate places, hyphens or em dashes are placed in the right places, and it reads with ease.

Investing in a professional interior designer is something that will make your book look professional from cover to cover. Beauty really is from the inside out.

If you never want someone to pick up your book and say, "Oh, you self-published," in a derogatory way, start your search for a great designer right now.

CHAPTER 15:

IS IT STILL READING IF YOUR AUDIENCE IS LISTENING?

In 2016, when I was about to launch my second book, *The New Brand You*, I hosted a two-day event in Vancouver to help folks in and around the real estate industry build their brand. People had flown in from all over the country, including one of my guest speakers and a videographer from San Diego.

The night before the event, I went to bed feeling off. I figured I'd eaten something bad and sure enough I threw up all night long. Registration was at 8:00 a.m., and while I had two volunteers helping with the event, I still had to show up. I showered, brushed my teeth three times, and got the event going.

On the second day, as we discussed how our brands reflect the ways we show up in the world, one of the attendees asked, "What if you just don't feel like it? You know, you don't feel like attending that event or making that call you know you should make?"

I laughed and said, "Do you know what happened to me yesterday? I think I ate something bad at dinner and…" It was fun watching their jaws drop as I revealed what I'd been through the day before and how I showed up without their having any idea. (By the way, I didn't know it at the time but it turns out I was pregnant and that was just the start of seven months of getting sick all the time!)

My "performance" the day before had been for them since they showed up for me, and while I felt off all day, focusing on delivering for them made me feel better too. I projected the excitement, belief, and positivity I wanted my audience to feel and little by little, despite barely any sleep and no food, I felt it too!

There's even scientific evidence to back that up. When someone modifies their own voice to sound a little happier and then hears it, they feel happier.[41] Conversely, you can also make yourself feel angrier or sadder with the same technique.

That's the power of your voice and your tone, apart from the actual words you say. A professional narrator should be able to do this with your audiobook but they are your words. Realistically, nobody can apply the right tone and emotion to your words as you. Given the level of trust and rapport that builds when you gain familiarity with a voice, why would you NOT record an audiobook? And, unless you have a good reason for not recording it yourself, that is what I would recommend.

Not only can audiobooks have brand-building benefits but they also are a source of increasing income for authors.

Audiobooks have had double-digit growth for seven years straight. It's now a $1 billion industry in the US with no sign of slowing down.[42]

---

41 Chau Tu, "The Emotive Power of Voice," Science Friday, February 10, 2016, https://www.sciencefriday.com/articles/the-emotive-power-of-voice/.

42 Adam Rowe, "U.S. Audiobook Sales Neared $1 Billion In 2018, Growing 25% Year-Over-Year," *Forbes*, July 16, 2019, https://www.forbes.com/sites/adamrowe1/2019/07/16/us-audiobook-sales-neared-1-billion-in-2018-growing-25-year-over-year/#768953ad6050.

The marketplace also is moving to audio and visual content. You might even be listening to this book right now, having thought that you wouldn't have the time or opportunity to read a hard copy.

The decision whether or not to record an audiobook is more complex than this, however. Audiobooks are expensive to produce in the quality that is expected by most consumers and by ACX, which is the company that puts books on Audible. Also, to achieve your specific goals, you may not need an audiobook.

Let's get into it so you make the right decision for your budget and book, shall we?

First, if you have the budget and belief in your message, the decision is simple in my mind: Produce an audiobook. Here are some of the reasons why:

1. There are far fewer audiobooks on the market than there are print books and e-books. It's easier to stand out and be found in your space because so much of your competition will never appear in an audio format (and there isn't the massive backlist of audiobooks that there are in e-book and print books).

2. It enhances your credibility and helps establish trust with your audience. When you see a book available in multiple formats, you assume the book is high quality. Going the extra effort will make you look that much more professional.

3. If you read your book yourself, your voice is now in the reader's head. Think about the podcasters you listen to on a regular basis. You really feel like some of them are friends, don't you? This is a really big opportunity for you to build a relationship with your reader.

4. Recording an audiobook is fun! You'll also be able to share some awesome social media posts and behind-the-scenes pics with your audience.

5. Reading your book aloud allows you to catch some little typos that may have been missed, no matter how many editors have worked on your book. Because you're self-publishing and likely using Print-On-Demand to produce your book, it's never too late to correct a typo!

LET'S TALK DOLLARS AND SENSE

For every hour of book recording, it actually takes a professional six to eight hours to edit and master the file. It requires someone with great equipment and an experienced ear. Depending on your narration speed, it's approximately one hour of audio for every 9,000 words. If your book is about 60,000 words, your audiobook will likely end up being roughly seven hours long. When you realize the hours that go into each finished hour, it doesn't seem as crazy that you have to spend somewhere around $300–$500 per finished hour for your book production!

For your own planning, to record your book, including tongue twisters, ums, misreads, energy drops, and dry mouth, it's going to take you at least twice the finished hours to record your book. In fact, I would plan for 2.5 times that.

If your book contains 60,000 words, I would reserve a studio for at least 14 hours but probably more like 16 hours. And if you think you're going to do two eight-hour days to knock it out, I wouldn't recommend it! It's far more taxing than you think. I'd recommend you schedule three days, each with six hours of recording time and several breaks.

PREPARING TO RECORD AN AUDIOBOOK

Can't you just grab a mic and hit record?

Many podcasters have decent equipment that would probably be sufficient to record an audiobook and some of our clients have made it work. My audiobook, *The New Brand You*, was recorded in a small room in my parents' house where we hung thick blankets all over the walls for soundproofing. I did many sound tests with my editor before I hit record. It was finnicky and took a lot of back and forth to set up. I would have rather used a professional studio but I was pregnant. I feared that being in a studio when morning sickness hit was going to be a big problem for me. I needed the flexibility of being at home.

It's simpler for many authors to just rent a studio and have a professional on-site to help everything go smoothly. It is, however, entirely possible to set it up at home as I proved. It just takes patience and some professional assistance to get rid of echoes and get the sound just right.

Audible has very strict quality standards and a lot of books are rejected for not meeting them. Even with professional production, we still get some books kicked back and have to make file edits.

If you're fine with skipping Audible and distributing in other ways, then nonprofessional audiobook production is a great option for you. It will still require editing but you can do it for much less. Be sure that's what you really want, though. If you're writing a book to enhance your reputation and credibility, you likely want to look like a polished professional.

Regardless of where you record, here are some tips to succeed:

1. Read your book aloud at least once before you record. **Make notes on how to pronounce names and places and add commas.** Commas mean "breathe." You won't really know where you'll get breathless unless you've done a practice run. This is also where you'll find stuff that you don't know whether to read or not (charts, graphs, footnotes, etc.), and you can make decisions in advance and not on the fly.

2. Record a chapter and run it by a voice coach. This is not the same as podcasting or public speaking. With an audiobook, every single word needs to be read, heard, and understood. A voice coach will also pick up on habits. You may not pronounce your Ts as well or you raise your voice at the end of sentences that are statements. A voice coach will help you with this. They'll also help you figure out when you should breathe if you're not getting it right.

3. On the day of recording, avoid any foods or drinks that will give you phlegm. That includes spicy foods and dairy products. Also avoid anything fizzy because you don't want to burp. And plan to keep hydrated. Tea with honey and lemon, hot water, and room temperature water are best. Bring snacks. If you're not sure what impacts your voice, test foods in the days leading up to your session and see what works. For me, unsalted nuts and fruit like apples and grapes work really well.

4. Keep Audible's rating system in mind when you're making your audiobook. Your listener will rate your book based on three factors: Overall quality. Performance. And story. Assuming you have a good book, audiobook success is a balance between a good recording, strong pacing, and great editing, with good mastering. And if you don't know what any of that means, that means you need help.

5. Have fun. This is your book and you're bringing it to life in an entirely new and cool way.

Oh, and even though you've recorded the entire book, you're not done. Prepare yourself for "pickups." They're spots where it's faster for an editor to rerecord your voice than to try to clean up the mess you made. The pickups are easy but it means you can't take down that home studio right away. You're going to have to do some parts over again, even if it's just two or three words.

WHERE TO HIRE YOUR AUDIOBOOK EDITOR

If you're not working with Book Launchers or a company like ours to produce your audiobook, you might be wondering where you hire a voice coach or a professional audiobook editor. If you aren't narrating it yourself, Findaway Voices has some great options for narrators and to get your audiobook produced. If you're narrating yourself, I recommend you join an author group on Facebook and ask your fellow authors whom they recommend. You can also hire audiobook editors via Upwork.com, Indeed, and guru.com, among other sites.

Some studios will do the editing right on-site, and that's often included in a package deal if you find a great studio. The challenge we've found is that a lot of studios aren't as good as you expect. In about 10–15 percent of the cases we've encountered, the studio is unable to produce the high level of quality needed for the audiobook. This is especially true of studios set up for music recording! Before you pay for an entire session, do a test session and make sure the quality is there.

AUDIOBOOK DISTRIBUTION

In North America, Audible is the big player, and if you go exclusively with ACX, which is Amazon's company, you get a bigger cut of the pie—a much bigger cut. With ACX, you can reach Audible, amazon.com, and Apple Books, and if you go with them exclusively, you'll earn a 40 percent royalty rate on every book sold.[43] If you aren't exclusive, you're only earning 25 percent. ACX also does not let you set your list price. You have no control over that so you can't raise your price to adjust your earnings. A longer book typically will be priced higher than a shorter book, but ACX does the calculation and adjusts it over time.

---

43 "How it Works: Authors," ACX, accessed September 8, 2020, https://www.acx.com/help/authors/200484540?utm_medium=author&utm_campaign=hiwtable.

For a straight up ROI consideration, if you are in the US reaching US listeners, going exclusive with Audible for the first year and then asking to be released from exclusivity to go wide might make the most sense. Being exclusive with ACX allows you to make more money but you are *limiting your distribution*. If you have international readers or you want your audiobook available in libraries, you won't want to be exclusive forever. At that point, you will want to consider an aggregator like Findaway Voices.

It is worth noting your exclusive contract with ACX is for seven years. But if you narrated your own book, ACX now offers release from that exclusivity after 90 days.

When you go wide with a service like Findaway Voices, you'll reach your readers wherever they are and open yourself up to new ways of promoting your book. In particular, you can look for services that partner with BookBub for Chirp distribution and promotion.

Whether you decide to do an audiobook or not isn't as simple as you think. The financial considerations are significant but the rewards are great. Your readers will have another way to connect with you, you'll have another income source from your book, and you will have a new experience in life!

CHAPTER 16:

HERE ARE SEVEN PLACES TO SELL BOOKS—ONLY ONE STARTS WITH AN "A"

After a great summer visiting family in Canada, my husband and I were driving back to our home in California. As we crossed into the United States, we were stopped by a border control agent, who asked me to show him the company financials for Book Launchers.

"If you can't show that your company is profitable, you're staying in Canada," the agent said.

This was completely unexpected.

I called our immigration lawyer who said I wasn't legally required to do this. At the same time, she advised we tread very carefully because we were, to a degree, at the mercy of the agent.

Rather than argue, I decided to gather the necessary documents. Of course, they wanted printed copies of everything. We had to cross into the US, put the financials on a USB, find a print shop, and then get back in line at the border to cross back into Canada. Once in Canada, we had to turn around and come back through the line to enter the US. We had to wait two hours to show the documentation to the agent. Then, we watched as this young guard poured over our financials before giving us the go ahead to return to the States.

If that sounds ridiculous, then you've read it right.

Did I mention we did this all in the heat of summer with a 2.5-year-old boy and our dog? My stress level was off the charts that day.

We were at the mercy of one agent who held our lives in his hand. As an author, it may feel as if you are at the mercy of one publisher, who holds the fate of your book in theirs: Amazon.

It's not exactly an apples-to-apples comparison but you get the point. And just like we could choose to live somewhere other than the US, you also have options. A lot of them.

Sure, many of your book sales ARE going to happen through Amazon, and independent authors have a lot to thank Amazon for. It leveled the playing field, making it possible for self-publishing authors to be as successful as traditionally published authors and make way more money!

But too much power in the hands of one company puts you in a challenging situation. What if that company decides to lower your royalty dramatically, won't promote your book for whatever reason, or just decides one day to stop selling it? When you rely on one company for all your income as an author, you set yourself up for potential problems.

The more you, as an author, support and encourage the sale of books through other avenues, the better off all authors will be.

It helps to understand your distribution alternatives (I'm a fan of wide distribution), but first you need to know how your book is going to be printed and made available because e-books aren't as popular for nonfiction as you might think. In fact, most of Book Launchers' clients sell more than 70 percent of their books in print, especially in the first three months after launch. The only time that didn't happen was when our client insisted on pricing her print editions about $10 higher than the market, which drove people to buy the e-version of the book instead.

You have two options for printing your book, if that's what you choose to do, and both are great.

PRINT-ON-DEMAND VS. OFFSET PRINTING

We live in a great era for publishing, perhaps the best. Gone are the days of storing 1,000 copies of your book in your garage.

At Book Launchers, we work with all formats of books for our clients, and nonfiction authors need to do both print books and e-books. We set them up with accounts at KDP for amazon.com distribution and IngramSpark for distribution everywhere else, including bookstores, Amazon in other countries, and more.

What people may not realize is IngramSpark and KDP are Print-On-Demand publishers. Print-On-Demand is exactly how it sounds. Using a digital file of your manuscript and cover, the book gets printed each time it's ordered.

The benefits of Print-On-Demand are pretty big:

- ✔ There's no warehouse required to store your books while you wait for them to sell.
- ✔ The speed is impressive. Less than one week after finishing your book, you can hold a copy in your hands.
- ✔ If you have to change your book for some reason, the change can take effect fairly quickly. One of our clients printed 3,000 books with offset printing and changed his book jacket after the books were printed. Since he had thousands of books already, the new book jacket couldn't be available until his next print run. Luckily for him, he quickly sold through all his copies but that's not always

the case. For many authors, selling 3,000 books could take a few years to happen, if at all.

✔ You create less waste.

Print-On-Demand is digital with ink. It's different than offset, which uses plates where inked images are transferred (or offset) from a plate to a rubber blanket then onto paper. The offset process is a lithographic process that's based on the repulsion of oil and water. (Check out YouTube for some explanatory videos.) The bottom line is, offset is geared for mass production and it's much cheaper if you're printing thousands and thousands of books, especially if you're printing in color.

As an example, let's take a typical 260-page nonfiction book. The Print-On-Demand cost would be roughly $4 per book. But if you need 10,000 copies, an offset printing run might cost you under $2 per book. You can enjoy a fairly significant savings with offset but where are you going to store 10,000 books until they sell?

For a wide print book distribution, upload your book to Ingram-Spark. While Amazon has "expanded distribution" and there are a few stories of authors who only publish with KDP who get their book into bookstores, those stories are few and far between. Bookstores don't want to do business with Amazon and give money to their biggest competitor, and they aren't given favorable prices to buy from Amazon's expanded distribution.

Also, if you want to pitch universities, colleges, and other retail outlets, you may be out of luck unless you set up consignment arrangements in each location. (Consignment, by the way, is a huge pain in the butt and expensive for an author because you buy the books, give them to the store, and get paid if and when they sell.)

THE BOOK LAUNCHERS DISTRIBUTION PLAN

This can get quite complex so let me just tell you how we handle it for our clients. We set our client's books up for distribution via:

- ✔ KDP Print for Amazon.com distribution with Kindle and Soft Cover Print
- ✔ IngramSpark for Amazon internationally, chain bookstores such as Barnes & Noble, major retailers like Walmart, and independent bookstores
- ✔ Draft2Digital to get widespread e-book distribution to reach global markets, Kobo readers, libraries via Hoopla, and an ever-expanding market of folks reading books digitally all around the world
- ✔ ACX for audiobooks on Audible
- ✔ Findaway Voices for audiobook distribution on Apple, libraries, Chirp (BookBub company), and international options for readers to find and listen to your audiobook
- ✔ Lulu to sell books on your website (or for ordering beautiful color versions of your book)

Selling books from your website can be a great way to make the most money and maintain your buyers' contact information. That said, selling a book direct from your website is a pain. Collecting payment, taxes, shipping, and other logistics can turn your garage into a warehouse and keep your kids employed on weekends. It's not my idea of a good time, so if you want a simple way to sell your book on your website with minimal hassle, Lulu has a great option.

Lulu (https://www.lulu.com) is a self-publishing and Print-On-Demand platform, and it's free to use. You upload your manuscript and cover and then you only have to pay when you print copies of your book. If you have specialty color books, in particular, their service is really great. They've also created an app for Shopify that allows you to sell directly to your readers.

You, as the author, keep 100 percent of the revenue and get transactional data. You can use this to build out your email list and help you market future books in smarter ways. If your book is $20 and it costs $5 to print, you'll get paid $15, though Shopify may charge transaction fees. (For more information about Lulu, check out our video at booklaunchers.com/notboring.)

E-BOOK DISTRIBUTION

Amazon Kindle definitely has the market for e-books cornered in the United States but it's not the only player in the marketplace. If you want to capture a big chunk of Canadian readers and other English speakers around the world, look at Kobo, and for library distribution, Hoopla and OverDrive. Some of these platforms (Kobo, Apple, Google Play) let you go direct to upload. But now you have a bunch of accounts to manage, track sales, and ultimately make changes if you adjust your book in any way. Plus, not all e-book distribution options have the option to go direct. Overdrive, which gets your e-book into the US library system, requires you use an aggregator service like Draft2Digital to access their service.

The downside of an aggregator like Findaway Voices for audiobooks or Draft2Digital for e-books is, of course, less money and a little less control. The upside is a whole lot of reduced pain in the patootie.

Working with an aggregator becomes one place to see your stats, one place to make updates, and one place to get paid. Also, they will reach a lot more readers than just the big players so you really can connect with people wherever they are looking for you. Of course, you pay them a fee for their services but that seems only fair.

Going direct or going through an aggregator is largely a choice of cost versus convenience, with personal control being a smaller but nevertheless important issue.

Whatever you decide, know this: it is not the job of Kobo, Kindle, Apple, or any distribution channel to sell your book.

It is your job to get your book in front of readers. Some of these companies do a better job of helping you with this than others, but distribution doesn't matter if you're not marketing your book.

GETTING INTO BOOKSTORES

As an author, there's nothing better than the feeling of walking into a bookstore and seeing your book on the shelf. It's pretty darn cool and it's especially such a delight when it's a surprise. Six years after my book, *More than Cashflow*, came out, I stumbled upon it in a store and felt a surge of joy. If you're smart, you'll buy that copy right away and rave to the cashier about the amazing author! You might feel silly but they'll remember it the next time someone is asking for a recommendation in that category.

Online book buying is where you'll find the majority of your readers but bookstore distribution is still valuable. A lot of people browse a bookstore when they have time and discover new books that way.

If you want your self-published book to have a shot at getting on the bookshelves of your local bookstore, or bookstores across the country, then you must do four things.

1. Upload your book to IngramSpark. Books published through that service are available through the Ingram Catalog, which is where bookstores will buy your book.

2. Buy your ISBN, or if you are lucky enough to be living in Canada, get your free ISBN.

3. Set your wholesale discount to 55 percent, which is the discount expected by bookstores. It reduces your profit, but if you don't do this, you won't get bookstore orders.

4. Make your books returnable. If your books are not returnable, bookstores will not order from you. Here's an expert tip: Under Return options, choose 'Yes—Destroy' as your option, not 'Yes—Deliver.' Don't opt to have them sent back to you because shipping is really expensive.

LOVE YOUR LOCAL LIBRARY

There are over 100,000 libraries in the United States.[44] That's a lot of places that could buy and stock your book. If you want to get that kind of widespread listing, you should do a few things first, including having your book listed in the Library of Congress. The listing isn't guaranteed, by the way, and you need to meet three criteria to apply:

1. Your book can't be published yet.

2. It has to be published in the United States and on your copyright page, you need to list the address of your office in the United States where they can send inquiries.

3. Your book must be available in print. An e-book-only version is not eligible.

If you meet those criteria, apply for a PCN, which is the Preassigned Control Number Program. It's the only option available to indie publishers. There are some exclusions, like mass-market trade paperbacks, textbooks, and magazines, so you'll have to determine if you still qualify.

For more detailed information, I highly recommend picking up a copy of David Wogahn's book, *Register Your Book: The Essential Guide to ISBNs, Barcodes, Copyright, and LCCNs*. It explains all this riveting stuff along with the application process, among other issues.

---

44 "Number of Libraries in the United States: Home," American Library Association, accessed September 8, 2020, https://libguides.ala.org/numberoflibraries.

Library listings in Canada and the US are possible without going through the above steps. It won't happen automatically though. You need to get the library to order your book.

At Book Launchers, we've had success with this in a variety of ways:

✔ Hosting events at local libraries. They almost always purchase a copy of your book if you host a live author event at their location.
✔ Get library card holders to request your book.
✔ Contact the library with a pitch sheet about why their local readers will want the book. This can work especially well if your book will tie in with a library theme such as Back to School, Halloween, Heart Health Month, and literacy promotion.
✔ Sell a lot of books so the demand is there, and the libraries will order it if it's a top seller in a category that has demand at their location.

Even for e-books, library distribution is primarily a curated process where local libraries choose whether to carry your digital book (through a system called Overdrive). But most important, you need to know you are only paid once for the purchase of that book or e-book that goes into the library.

That's the thing many people don't realize: even if your book is borrowed 100 times, you generally get paid exactly once.

Hoopla is different. It's an online platform that allows library users to borrow e-books and audiobooks. Unlike a normal library listing, however, Hoopla Digital pays a nominal fee per download. This means you don't get full royalties on the first borrow, but it also means that if 100 people borrow your book, you are making way more than you would normally through a library listing.

UNCONVENTIONAL BOOK MARKETS—INDIRECTLY TO YOUR READER

My first book was about real estate, and I sold a lot of books directly to real estate associations, mortgage brokers, and realtors who wanted to give it as a gift to their clients. I ordered the books by the case and shipped them to their offices. Sometimes they wanted signed copies, which took more coordination.

This should get you thinking: who has your reader in their client base?

You just might find a partner in promotion, or even better, a bulk buyer for your book if you help their clients with a problem they don't solve!

If you're an accountant who writes a book on how to understand the financials of your online business, a perfect promotional partner is a business coaching company that serves online businesses. Perhaps, you have a gardening book that talks about a tool to make planting your garden easier every year. That tool company may want to offer your book at an upcoming convention as a free gift with a tool purchase. If you have a book on running tips, your local running store might carry it.

Get creative because there are many places that will carry your book. My dentist office and my CrossFit gym, for instance, both sold copies of my second book because they wanted to support their client!

As an independent author, you might struggle to find large chains that will carry your book, which I hope doesn't discourage you. We thought we were getting a client's book into CVS pharmacy, for example, until they found out the book wasn't from a major publisher. They said indie authors don't do enough marketing and they need the push that comes with traditionally published books to move them off their shelves.

I disagree, and we work with a handful of traditionally published authors who use us JUST for marketing, but it was a pretty firm policy. In the future, I think we would try again, especially if a book is selling well enough and we're getting major media attention for it.

At the same time, smaller chains and independent stores are often really excited to support local authors, and who knows? You might find the perfect audience for your book. This goes for airport bookstores too. Our client, Gautam Baid, got his book, *The Joy of Compounding*, into Omaha airport bookstores just by speaking to the store managers. And Robert Workman, author of *Hired Gun II*, has systematically landed every major US airport as a distributor for his book. (You can watch his author spotlight video at booklaunchers.com/notboring.)

BACK OF THE ROOM SALES ARE BIG BUCKS IN YOUR POCKET

If you're invited to speak but they aren't paying you, ask to get a table at the back of the room where you can sell your book. The opportunity to sell your book for cash is a tremendous opportunity for you to move dozens, even hundreds of books. Live appearances and events are great book movers.

I'm not a fan of your handing books out for free at events. I've gone to conferences where authors with backpacks full of books literally hand them out to everyone they meet, and when the author walks away, people awkwardly decide whether to throw the book out or give it to someone else. Let's face it, free books are only valuable if you are actually interested in them. And as soon as someone gives you something unsolicited for free, you find it even less valuable, right?

For now, all I want you to do is think about how you can incorporate your book into events you attend. Maybe you give the organizers a copy for every attendee in exchange for sponsorship? Possibly, they buy a copy for every attendee in exchange for your talk or some other promotional service.

Books can be used as currency if you've created a great book that people value. And you can profit from it in many ways.

ONE OF THE MOST POWERFUL PAGES YOU CAN PUT IN A BOOK

A single page in your book could generate thousands of books sales: the marketing page.

This is the page you put at the back of your book with the primary goal of selling it in bulk.

Here's what you need to say on this simple page:

> *Interested in buying 10 or more copies? Call us for our discount schedule.*
>
> *Phone Number*
>
> *Email Address*

That's it!

You can get a little fancier with your call to action, but essentially you want the readers of your book to know that you can sell them your book in BULK. You see, an executive at a company may read your book on virtual meeting success and realize every person in her company needs a copy of the book, but she doesn't want to pay the Amazon price of $23 per book for 1000 copies. This single page may be the inspiration she needs to reach out and strike a deal.

Bulk sales are a huge opportunity to get a lot of your books into the hands of people who will benefit. It also offers self-published authors an advantage because you can make up your own discount schedule and don't have someone else setting the price of your book.

Here's what I would probably do if your book is selling for $17.99–$20.00 (USD) retail:

10–50 copies: $12 + shipping

50–100 copies: $10 + shipping

100–500 copies: $8.50 + shipping

500+ copies: $7.00 + shipping

This assumes your costs are roughly $4.00–$5.00 per printed book but that depends on the size of the book, color printing, and more.

You could also sell your book at a price that includes free shipping.

But that's not really the point. The point is that you need a page in your book for your reader to realize that every single person in their business or industry also needs to read it—and they want to gift it to them or simply spread the word!

This won't be every reader but there might be one or two who order 100 or 1,000 copies of your book. You won't know who they are but some of them just might run big companies, head a cool organization, or have a big social media following. In fact, when you think about avid readers in the world, they often are EXACTLY the kinds of people who have the power and influence to get your book out in a big way!

By the way, the end of your book is also a great place to share that you are available for speaking engagements. **Often, the best bulk buy deals involve your giving a lecture or talk, where people are able to purchase your book.**

The bottom line is, you have multiple options for selling your book. Amazon has given us a great gift as indie authors but you don't need to give them all the power over your book or your author business.

CHAPTER 17:

AMAZON ISN'T GOING TO SELL YOUR BOOK FOR YOU

"Holy shit, Julie—you did it! Your book is #1 on Amazon."

The moment my book topped the charts on Amazon is one I won't forget. After Wiley had turned me down, saying that I didn't have a strong enough marketing platform to sell books, my victory was all the sweeter. I took a niche nonfiction real estate book, self-published it, and outsold Dan Brown and the *Game of Thrones!*

Most authors can't say their book reached #1 on Amazon, and I'm incredibly proud of that.

But Oprah didn't call. I didn't get to dance with Ellen. I made some great money but I did not get rich.

Getting my book on Amazon was not enough.

Too many authors think Amazon is going to launch their book into the stratosphere and then wonder why they've sold less than 100 copies in a year.

There is so much work to selling books on Amazon. Here's five things that you need to do once your book is available there:

1. **Do keyword and category research** before you write your description. (See the note below on BISAC codes for choosing the appropriate categories.) For keywords, make sure you're getting the relevant keywords that people are searching for and that ideally you aren't competing with dozens of big selling books. (See my earlier advice on keywords for specific guidance.)

2. **Get reviews.** Verified purchase reviews are the absolute best, but you can still give out free books and ask for an honest review in exchange for a free copy. Spread the book around to clients, colleagues, associates, and ask them to read it and write a review. A lot of people will happily take that free book but about 20–30 percent will actually write reviews, even if you follow up and ask them politely to come through on their commitment. Know going in that you're going to have to get commitments from a lot of people.

3. **Submit your book to the LOOK INSIDE program.** If you haven't submitted a Kindle version of your book, which automatically creates this LOOK INSIDE feature for you, then you need to submit your book to the LOOK INSIDE program. Go to "Search Inside! Publisher Sign-Up" and then LOOK INSIDE will be activated on your Books Main Detail page within 7–10 days after you complete the content submission. This feature allows someone to click on your book in Amazon and preview the first 10 percent or a randomized page selection including up to 80 percent of the book (you set the percentage). This is why we spent so much time earlier in this book talking about why you need to make the first pages of your book AMAZING!

4. **Create your author page on Amazon Central.** It gives you the opportunity to upload extra pictures, your biography, vid-

eos, blogs, and more details about your book. As you write more books, you can add them here too. It's a great way for customers to find you in a different spot on Amazon.

5. **Start learning Amazon Ads,** and after you've completed the previous steps and have at least a dozen reviews, start running ads. While this book isn't going to go into detail on advertising, Amazon Ads has a lot of good resources, and it's really a great way to get your book seen.

THE ESSENTIALS ON BOOK METADATA

Whenever we have a new hire on our team, we put up a slide on our daily huddle that says, "Welcome to the nerd zone." We're self-proclaimed book nerds, to one degree or another. It's embedded in the culture of Book Launchers so deeply that the requirement to love books and their authors is in our job descriptions.

Being book nerds means that we get crazy excited about data-driven decision-making and advertising. We also geek out on book metadata in a way that would drive a normal person crazy.

All that is to say, I'm going to try to keep this simple, but you need to understand the importance of book metadata.

Here's what you need to know: Search engines use metadata to help readers and others online, including bookstores, chains, and wholesalers find your book. In other words, this is all about discoverability.

If you want Amazon to even have a shot at selling your book for you, this is essential.

Metadata includes:

- Title
- Subtitle
- Price
- Page count

- Trim size
- ISBN
- Author name
- Genre keywords
- Categories
- Book format of the book
- Other special details, including who wrote the foreword, your book description, and reviews of your book.

It's also worth considering issues such as whether your book takes place in a certain time period. For example, we have a memoir set during World War II and another book about a serial killer in a certain decade from a particular geographic area. Those are all details that should be in your metadata.

Maintaining fresh, relevant metadata is one of those things you can do over time to keep your book in front of new potential readers. We discuss metadata at BookLaunchers.TV and at booklaunchers.com/notboring and IngramSpark has some great info on their website as well.[45]

BISAC CODES

BISAC codes are an important part of getting your book set up for success as a self-publishing author.

The BISAC code is essentially a code that tells retailers, sellers, buyers, search engines, and libraries your book genre.

It's a way to categorize your book.

Let's say you are Marc Megna, who wrote the incredibly inspiring book *Dream Big, Never Quit*. You are totally fine with being #1 in Football Biographies (nice work, Marc!) but you don't

---

45   Carla King, "The Basics of Book Metadata and Keywords," IngramSpark, November 8, 2016, https://www.ingramspark.com/blog/the-basics-of-book-metadata-and-keywords.

want to end up in Sports Fiction or Personal Finance books.

The people looking for those books aren't interested in your book.

So how do you select the right BISAC code? Well, first you should know that when you upload to a system like IngramSpark or KDP Print, only one code is required but you're better off selecting three. It's unlikely your book touches on only one subject, and you can definitely appeal to people in more than one category.

The first one code should be the most precise, focused on your main topic. And ideally, it should be the most specific. Codes range from categories such as Antiques & Collectibles to Business & Economics, Education, Medical, and True Crime. Within those categories are many more subcategories.

The latest BISAC Codes can be found here: https://bisg.org/page/bisacedition.

A quick note: Amazon's category list doesn't match with any industry standard categorization, and Amazon.ca or Amazon.UK are different than Amazon.com.

The BISAC codes also are important because Amazon accepts your first two BISAC codes and uses them to determine the closest matches to Amazon categories. Additionally, Amazon also uses your keywords to put your book in the most accurate "browse category."

If you ever wonder why your book has landed in a funky category that's way off your topic, then you need to review the BISAC categories and keywords to see why Amazon thought your book was a fit.

Here's a couple of tips:

- Select categories that apply to your book as a whole—not only individual chapters.

- Try not to ever use the GENERAL category as it's...well, general.

Be consistent with your BISAC across different formats. In other words, the BISAC for your e-book should be the same as your print and audiobooks.

THE POWER OF PRESALE

We recommend our clients have their book complete and uploaded at least six weeks prior to their book launch. It's a period of time, called presale, where your book can be purchased but it's not yet available to read. Presale allows you time to sort out the inevitable kinks that can arise with the various catalogs and plays a very important part in laying a strong marketing foundation for your book.

Unless you work with a company like Book Launchers that oversees the process, it's your job to make sure you've set up your book correctly on Amazon, Barnes & Noble, Chapters Indigo, Kobo, Apple, or wherever your book is going to be available. We've seen all kinds of weird errors like the wrong book cover on an author's book, the wrong interior, pricing issues, and typos on one platform that aren't on another. You have to make the corrections to these issues, and it's much better to do that when it's in prelaunch than when you have hungry readers trying to buy your book and finding all kinds of problems.

A presale period is optional, though. If you're doing only Amazon distribution via KDP, you can upload a book and have it for sale pretty much 48 hours later.

If you're uploading to IngramSpark, you need more time to allow the catalogs to populate—especially if you're planning promotions that include bookstores online or in person. Typically, for example, Canadian bookstores and even Amazon in other countries will take a full six weeks to properly get the information on your book in their system. If you look at traditionally published books, they often have the book done six months in advance to allow adequate time for prelaunch activities, including distribution setup and promotion.

If having things right is important and you want to have a successful book launch, you need a presale period of six to eight weeks.

Besides making sure details are right, your presale time is an opportunity to build a foundation of success for your book's launch. And depending on the goals of your book launch and your book marketing, you should spend a minimum of two weeks and as much as three months in presale.

What are you doing during this presale period? Here are my recommendations:

1. Make sure the distribution is set up, pricing is right, and your book is where it should be.

2. Sell copies to your early reviewers at a discount. You can lower the price to $2.99 and have your book army and supporters buy the book on Amazon so they can post verified reviews.

3. Know that the longer your book is available for preorder, the more time you have to send readers to Amazon and other stores to buy the print books. This can help with your stock and your bestseller rankings.

   If your readers are buying print copies, these presale orders all add up and count as sales when the book ships out, which gives you a good chance at cracking some Top 100 subgenre lists on sites like Barnes & Noble and Apple. If readers buy on Amazon, it counts the day the purchase is made. If you're selling the e-version of your book on Kobo, the sale counts twice. It doesn't pay you twice but the sale counts for a presale ranking and then it counts on launch too. That's fun.

4. Remember that presales help prevent inventory shortages on launch day. If you have a killer launch and Amazon shows your book as temporarily out of stock, you'll lose sales! You'll also get a lot of complaints if you have hungry fans. Your readers can still purchase your book but sometimes Amazon is going to tell them the title will ship in four to six weeks. You do not want that. Presales volume tells Amazon to back that truck up and fill the warehouse so they've got inventory. In-stock titles are listed as available and ship immediately, and that's what you want.

For our latest recommendations on what to do during presale watch the video at booklaunchers.com/notboring

AMAZON REVIEWS – A QUICK TIP TO PREVENT REMOVAL

Reviews matter a lot in buying decisions and you need good, honest reviews. Every now and again, Amazon ends up doing a huge purge of what their bots determine are not legit reviews. They clean out a lot of bad reviews but legit reviews are always taken down with them. If you complain, you might get some of those reviews back. But it's a good idea to know the policy around the reviews to set yourself up to avoid this in the future.

Amazon does not want your friends and family to review your book. Friends and family are biased. But how does Amazon know who your friends and family members are? They own Goodreads after all, and one of the main ways to sign into Goodreads is via Facebook. Sign up for Amazon with a different email address than you use for social media or Goodreads, and don't connect your Goodreads account to social media when given the option.

EXCLUSIVE FOR E-BOOKS MIGHT WORK FOR YOU —WHAT YOU NEED TO KNOW ABOUT KDP SELECT

If maximizing your income from your book is more important than wide distribution, you may want to understand more about Amazon's KDP Select program.[46]

Amazon has created the KDP Select program for selling e-books in their Kindle store. It gives authors the opportunity to reach more readers and potentially make more money as part of their Kindle Unlimited program.

When you join, KDP will include your e-book in their Kindle Unlimited (KU)[47] and Kindle Owner's Lending Library (KOLL)[48] programs. KU is an international book subscription service that allows readers to read as many books as they like and keep them as long as they like for a monthly rate. KOLL is an international library where readers can select one book a month to read for free.

It does require exclusivity for your e-book, which is not something I love, but you can sell your print book and audiobook as widely as you want. If you choose KDP Select, you agree that your e-book is sold exclusively with Amazon for the next 90 days. That means you can't sell your book on your website or through Apple Books, Kobo, Overdrive, or Nook—only Amazon Kindle.

If your Kindle Unlimited readers review your book, it's not considered a "Verified Review" because they borrowed the book and did not pay for it. KU borrows add to paid purchase ranks and top categories ranks but it's not considered a purchase for a review.

You will be paid based on pages read. The calculation of how much

---

46 "KDP Select," Kindle Direct Publishing, accessed September 4, 2020, https://kdp. amazon.com/en_US/help/topic/G200798990.

47 "Kindle Unlimited," Kindle Direct Publishing, accessed September 4, 2020, https:// kdp.amazon.com/en_US/help/topic/G200798990.

48 "Kindle Owners' Lending Library," Kindle Direct Publishing, accessed September 4, 2020, https://kdp.amazon.com/en_US/help/topic/G200798990.

you're paid per page changes slightly month to month but it averages about \$0.0045 per page read. **There's a lot of nuances to this so go to the KU page on Amazon's website to investigate, but they also give you options to run a Kindle Countdown Deal or run a Free Book Promotion.**

Both of these promotions can create excitement around your book, and paired with a marketing ad in the right newsletter, they can help you get exposure. Because you only have to be exclusive for 90 days, this might be a great launch strategy for you with Amazon and then you can go wide afterwards. It can make a lot of sense of North American authors, in particular, to generate a lot more revenue from your launch promotions.

I'm not a fan of giving Amazon all the power over your business, but they are a powerhouse of promotional tools and reader reach that every author should understand and maximize to create success.

Amazon wants you to sell your book but you have to set it up for success. In order for the Amazon algorithm to help you, you need to implement the essential pieces that make it obvious who your book is for. Amazon is not much different than any other space for selling books in that you absolutely need a great title with a subtitle that clearly shows what benefit is inside for the reader. You also need an eye-catching cover, and then you need to focus on those early pages for reader previews. With features like "Look Inside," it's important to make sure you have a book description, table of contents, and must-read first pages that engage readers and make them curious about your book.

And, of course, getting the category selection and keyword selection right is important.

But none of that matters without massive support and effort by you, the author, to spread the word about the book.

CHAPTER 18:

WHAT YOU NEED TO KNOW ABOUT BEING A BESTSELLER

Were you last to be picked for a team in your phys ed class? When I was in elementary school, I wanted to run and hide whenever team captains were asked to choose their teams.

I was a nerdy know-it-all who loved school, not sports. And, six weeks into second grade, my teachers and parents made the decision to advance me to third grade to give me more of an academic challenge. I couldn't physically keep up with kids a year older than me. I wasn't popular and I wasn't an advantage on a sports team—so I was always picked last.

I was pretty lonely for a few years as I adjusted to the change of being moved up a grade. And maybe that is why I kind of resent some of the bestseller lists. You have to be chosen. *People decide whether you are cool enough to even be on a list, regardless of your qualifications.* Making a bestseller list doesn't have as much to do with your sales as you might think!

When it comes to *The New York Times*, those rules are based first on curation before actual sales. In other words, you need to be **selected** to be on that list as much as you need to sell a lot of books. As a self-publishing author, you should probably not spend your time focusing on *The New York Times* because it's *extremely* rare that an author outside of a major publishing house ever makes their list.

The good news is that there are many, many ways to become a best-selling author and sell a lot of books.

You just need to know the rules of the game because every list has some game elements.

HOW BESTSELLERS ARE CHOSEN

The Wall Street Journal uses the Nielsen Book Scan, a data provider for the book publishing industry owned by the Nielsen company. Book Scan compiles point-of-sale data for book sales. It covers print sales, including Amazon, but only if you publish with Ingram because Ingram reports back to Nielsen.

Barnes & Noble, Hastings, Target, Walmart, Costco are all places that report back to Nielsen Book Scan. To qualify for *The Wall Street Journal* list, you'll likely need to shoot for selling at least 5,000 books through retailers that report to Nielsen Book Scan each week. You might be able to do it for less, and it might take more sales, depending on the hot titles you're up against in any given week.

If you want to make *The Wall Street Journal* list, you'll need to ignore my earlier distribution advice because that is set up to maximize your revenue through KDP Print for Amazon.com. Books sold through KDP Print may not count.

USA Today, in contrast, ranks all print and e-book sales from select groups of booksellers in one massive list.

Meanwhile, Amazon updates their lists every hour based on real-time sales on their site. They rank books based on each type of book—not lumped together. So even though they have the same title, your e-book, audiobook, and print book will all be ranked as though they are each their own product. One of the reasons my book, *More than Cashflow*, topped the charts on Amazon was that I only had the print book for sale. I also drove people to buy on Amazon specifically. We had incentives for purchase during launch week that were only valid if you made a purchase on Amazon. I released the e-book a few weeks later.

I don't actually recommend you do this just to get a bestseller ranking. I am certain I lost a lot of sales not having the Kindle version of my book available at the same time. When someone wants to buy your book in an e-book or audio format and it's not available, sometimes they move on and forget about your book.

If you want to learn all about Amazon rankings and how to top the charts and consistently get Amazon to sell your book, check out a great book called *Amazon Decoded: A Marketing Guide to the Kindle Store* by David Gaughran.

But here's the thing, my future best-selling author friend, none of those sales are bulk sales. We've seen many authors sell thousands of books but not top the charts anywhere because corporations and associations bought their book by the hundreds. And that doesn't count on any list, anywhere.

When your sales are spread evenly across formats and outlets, you may also not make a list.

Best-selling book rankings is a game. Like any game, you can play to win and that's totally cool. I'm a fan of games, and I am a bigger fan of winning games. Sure, there's fun in playing but the real joy is in victory for me. That's why I say first you have to define what being a bestseller means to you and then decide the game you want to play.

Whether you choose to become a bestseller or you just want to sell a lot of books, there are three ways you can drive a lot of book sales.

THREE WAYS TO BECOME A BESTSELLER

Author Platform

An author platform is really a fancy way of having a place to say what you want to say and having people who listen. It's everything you do that puts you in front of an audience. It includes how many people see what you do, how often that gets shared, and the communities to which you belong.

One of the reasons Wiley rejected my book deal in Canada was that I wasn't part of a particular real estate network. My friends who got deals were all a part of that huge network. Even though I actually had a strong following of my own, Wiley likely felt that this real estate network was going to be the deal maker, or in my case, breaker. I proved them wrong, but the right community behind you can make your book sell if you're visible and involved.

Other parts of your platform include:

- Speaking engagements
- YouTube audience and engagement
- Social media following and engagement
- An email newsletter list
- Client base
- Anywhere you have an audience, including online posts, guest appearances and interviews, or places where you otherwise share your expertise.

Most platforms don't appear overnight. It takes discipline and consistency. The best day to start building your platform was yesterday, which means you need to start today.

You may wonder if you should wait until you have a platform before you publish. If you don't have one already, I wouldn't let that hold you back. A book is also a great way to grow a platform. But not having a platform will impact your ability to be a bestseller out of the gate.

If you have a platform, you should expect 0.1–0.5 percent of your social media following to buy your book, depending on the engagement level of your following.

Yes, that means the 10,000 Facebook fans on your page are likely to result in fewer than 50 book sales. And, honestly, that might be high. Some of our authors with highly engaged Instagram fans have enjoyed a higher percentage of book buying, but most of our clients see closer to 0.1 percent of their social media audience making a purchase.

If you have an engaged newsletter audience, you might see 5 percent of your subscribers buying your book when you launch, but if you haven't engaged with your list much or your open rates are less than 25 percent, then you are probably more likely to see 1 percent of your email list buying your book. Depending on the fit for the audience, it's possible that if you're selling books on-site, around 30 percent of any of your live audiences will buy your book.

Many authors never get on a bestseller list with their existing audience alone. But sales of your next book might perform much better if you do a good job of building a relationship with book buyers, so make sure you're building that audience with this book for future sales!

What can you do to build your platform?

Here's one idea: Start writing articles for websites or online magazines related to your publishing space. Include a short call to action at the end for readers to connect with you on your website or, ideally, subscribe to your newsletter.

Here's another idea: Release new quality content on your own blog, YouTube channel, and/or social media site every single week. My videos come out every Tuesday and Friday, and you can subscribe to catch them all. Consistency is critical. Produce content at first even if nobody is reading, listening, or watching, but do it over and over on a regular basis. When I began BookLaunchers.TV (our YouTube channel), I didn't post on a schedule. As a result, the channel growth and engagement were slow.

I watched what successful YouTubers were doing and noticed most published videos on a schedule so I started doing Fridays. Growth on the channel was still slow so I added Tuesdays to boost engagement and livestreams every other week. Voila! The channel eventually began to attract 1,000 new subscribers a month.

For most people, it takes years to build traction, but you'll get it if you create content that speaks directly to your audience and adds value.

My favorite way—and the fastest way—for most folks to build a platform is to step onto a stage and start speaking. This is the single best way to build a brand, and a business, and sell books. Launching into speaking is much easier when you have a book but you don't have to wait until your book is out. Once you know the hook of your book, it can be the hook of your pitch to speak at local MeetUp groups and associations—great places for new speakers to start out.

Finally, when you've written one book and plan to write another, give your audience ways to connect with you. I'm not talking about a link to your website. I'm talking about inviting your readers to download something of value in exchange for their email address. This is about building that audience and relationship so they might buy your next book or purchase your product or service.

Author platform building takes time, but the key to this is consistency. Keep going. Look at what works and do more of it. Look at what doesn't work and do less of it, and over time, you'll build a platform.

Other People's Platforms

A lot of people make the big lists by relying on the platforms of other people. They get influential friends, coworkers, colleagues, and acquaintances to promote their book all at the same time, during the same week. Often there's an incentive for buying the book then, and it's a great strategy to get books sold.

For example, with my book, *More than Cashflow*, Greg Habstritt, the author of *The RRSP Secret*, generously gave me his online course on investing your retirement funds in real estate to give away during the book launch week. The course was $299 normally and fit perfectly with the material in my book so to be able to give it away with the purchase of three books was a huge incentive. I'm still incredibly grateful he shared that with me as it was a big part of my book launch success. The high-value giveaway not only got my email subscribers to buy the book but it made it easy for my friends with their own audiences to share as well. Everyone looks like a hero when they share something of value.

You may think you don't have people who will share your message but think again. Almost every author we've met has connections that could serve as great promotional partners. Think about the creative places we discussed when it came to distribution. These are the places that might be promotional partners with their newsletter, podcast, or other audience connector methods. Maybe there's a product or person you mention favorably in your book. Perhaps, they will want to promote your book because it makes them look good too? Ideally, you have supported their business or platform in some way before you reach out, but no matter what, you have to be willing to ask for some support.

Because you've written a book that is of high value with a clear hook for a specific audience, you may be surprised at how supportive some people are about sharing your book with their audience. If you make someone say, "Oh my goodness, my clients NEED that book," you are much more likely to get support even if you don't have a strong relationship with them. Start brainstorming!

Pay to Play

If you don't have any influential friends or a platform of your own, then you have to buy your way onto a list. This can literally be done by hiring a company with an army of people all over the country who will go into the stores and buy your book.

According to *Forbes*, the cost of buying your way onto *The New York Times'* Bestseller list or *The Wall Street Journal* in 2013 was $100,000.[49] And some authors with deep pockets and the desire to be number one have been known to do this.

You can do this on a smaller scale by using paid promotions on Facebook, Google, Amazon, BookBub, Net Galley Reviews, Goodreads Giveaways, Book Sirens, and others. If you have a smart marketing mind and a juicy budget, you can get those ads flowing and ramped up to spark enough sales in a week to nail one of the major bestseller lists.

Of course, there are hundreds of ways to sell books, and it's going to take an entire book on marketing to help you navigate how to create a strategy and generate sales, but please know that these three things are the foundation of success: **You need to tell people about your book, ask for support, and try to create value for all the people with whom you connect.** It takes work, and it's not going to be easy, but you didn't become an author because it's the easy path, did

---

49 Jeff Bercovici, "Here's How You Buy Your Way Onto *The New York Times* Bestsellers List," *Forbes*, February 22, 2013, https://www.forbes.com/sites/ jeffbercovici/2013/02/22/heres-how-you-buy-your-way-onto-the-new-york-times- bestsellers-list/#71d8548a3a7b.

you? You did it to have an impact and build your ability to earn an income while having that impact, right?

The big thing with selling books for bestseller lists is coordinated timing of sales. Most of us will need to provide some sort of incentive to drive people to buy during a particular period of time in order to hit these lists. This takes a lot of effort and it's why most people hire a company like Book Launchers if they're really serious about selling books. It's also why I think you should focus on selling books to your ideal reader and if you top the charts while focusing on selling to your ideal reader, it's a bonus. Though I know from personal experience it sure can be fun to top the charts, even if Ellen and Oprah don't call.

CHAPTER 19:

BEATING BREAKEVEN

A re you going to make any money as an author?

I know it's on your mind. And it should be.

According to a study by The Authors Guild, about one quarter of all published authors surveyed in the US did not earn any money from book publishing in 2017.

But that same report said, "While self-published authors were the only group to experience a significant increase (up 95 percent in book-related income from 2013 to 2017), *self-published authors as a whole still earned 58 percent less than traditionally published authors in 2017.*[50]

The thing that this report doesn't say is that **self-published authors make far more money per book** sold and have the opportunity to leverage their book into massive income elsewhere. While that is also true of a traditionally published author, they have a lot more limitations than self-published authors. Remember my friend who had to buy his book back to work on that TV opportunity?

---

50 "Six Takeaways from the Authors Guild 2018 Author Income Survey," The Authors Guild, accessed September 4, 2020, https://www.authorsguild.org/industry-advocacy/six-takeaways-from-the-authors-guild-2018-authors-income-survey/.

Your book can become the starting place for you to make a lot of money if you choose to use it that way.

The one thing I can tell you with certainty is that success is never guaranteed. You're taking a risk when you write and publish a book.

One of the reasons I started Book Launchers was because I saw authors putting in a lot of effort to write and publish a book that ended up doing nothing. They didn't sell copies and they derived little benefit from being an author. What almost all of them had in common was what you have already learned: to develop a reader-focused book with a clear hook that positions you to achieve your goals.

It's never a certainty but we've seen some wonderful success stories. Jim Huddle wanted to warn people that they may not know a serial killer is in their midst. He wanted to tell them how he had no idea The Golden State Killer was in his family for decades. He didn't want a platform of his own to sell it, though—he just wanted the story out there. *Killers Keep Secrets* was born, and the television programs *20/20, Inside Edition,* and *Good Morning America* all featured him and his book on their shows.

Ben Preston didn't have an audience or a business but wanted to use his book to build both. He wrote a great book called *Harness Your Butterflies* to help millennials develop an exciting career plan. The book is leading to corporate training, panels, and he's starting to build an entire coaching business around it. You can see the video (booklaunchers.com/notboring) he did with us that reveals the cool opportunities he's uncovered as a result.

Jeremy Moore wanted a book to give his clients while at the same time sharing a message of hope to folks that struggle to put on muscle. *Trail Map to Muscles: How to Defeat Genetics, Disease, and Build A Confident Body* was his solution. The book become an additional income stream for his training business, marketing for that business, and a way for him to expand his impact beyond his current audience.

Many folks come into the book writing journey looking for a return on their investment through book sales. It's possible to sell enough books to make a return, but you're going to make a lot more money and a lot faster if you focus on getting a return on your book in other ways.

And straight up, I have to tell you that some of our clients haven't seen a great return on their book investment. Despite the best efforts of everyone involved, sometimes it happens that a book falls flat. Sometimes our clients decide not to follow our advice too. What can we do about that?! It's their book so they have the final say.

I'm sure the risk scares you but know that nothing great happens in the world, or your life, when you take the safe route. Taking smart risks is the way to provide a return beyond your wildest dreams. And sometimes you just have to write the first book to make room for the next book, which will be your great success.

Following the steps and tips in this book will set you up for a better chance at success when you go to market your book. If you make your book engaging, interesting, and reader-focused, you are going to be better positioned than 80 percent of the self-published books hitting the market today.

For now, let's walk through how you can pay for your book and start making a return right away.

SEVEN WAYS TO MAKE MULTIPLE STREAMS OF INCOME FROM YOUR BOOK:

1. **An Online Course**

   If you put all your best information in your book, will someone still buy your course?

   The answer is YES! In fact, you'll find folks are even more enthusiastic about your course as a result of reading your book. The thing to remember is a book is designed for consumption and a course is designed for action and results. That difference means your course may contain the same material but it should be organized differently to support those action-oriented student goals.

Years ago, I read the book *Pitch Anything* by Oren Klaff. At the time, my husband and I were buying houses every month and raising capital to fund those deals because the banks wouldn't loan us money. The book spoke precisely to our biggest challenges with the pitches we made to potential investors. And I wanted more! I wanted to absorb every lesson he taught. When his course came out for $299, it was obviously the same content as the book in a course format with videos and worksheets, and I was excited. I wanted another way to learn this material and put it into action.

The courses I built after *More than Cashflow* launched contained the same material but I added a weekly Q&A call. I sold the course for $697, eventually raising the price to $999. I also had a corresponding mastermind group that priced at $10,000 a year. After someone read my book, they could sign right up.

Typically, a course involves audio or visual material with downloadable resources. You can add live components if you want. The advantage of adding live components is that you can ask a higher price for the added value. Even without the live component, the different formats offer a whole new value proposition. Authors who invest sufficient time and energy in creating effective books are generally successful at attracting people to their related courses.

Most nonfiction books (not memoirs, but business, self-help, fitness, and health-related books) lend themselves beautifully to membership platforms, online or live courses.

2. **Consulting**

Telling people in great detail what they need to do will only make them want you to do it for them or, at the very least, guide them through it. Even though most problems can be resolved with similar processes and approaches, people tend to think their situations are unique and require personalized support. With many nonfiction book topics, you can most certainly expect people to call you and say, "Can I hire you to [fill-in-the-blank]?"

Start thinking right now about your hourly rate because there's a good chance you'll be asked.

3. **Speaking Gigs Part I**

Being a paid speaker is the goal of many authors and a book is likely to lead you toward that path. Many events look specifically for authors as their speakers. But being paid for speaking isn't the only way to generate revenue from speaking.

This is a two-parter because your book can get you booked for speaking gigs, and if you are smart, you can leverage those speaking gigs—even unpaid ones—into a lot of revenue.

If you want to be paid to speak, you may need to start with unpaid gigs. Get those filmed so you can begin building a speakers reel. Develop a few signature talks that will help you position yourself in the speakers market. And say yes to as many gigs as you can until you have a reputation as a good speaker. We have more videos on speaking to help you on BookLanchers.TV.

If you've already been speaking, don't be surprised when you find more opportunities and higher prices coming your way post book launch.

4. **Book Sales with Speaking Gigs Part II**

   You can also use your book as an add-on to increase your speaking or workshop fees. If you're already getting paid to speak, you can now offer a second contract option that includes the sale of your book to the audience. Many companies accept the talk fee + book sale option and generate additional revenue for you.

   If you're new to speaking, you might be able to negotiate an option to sell your book at the back of the room or for organizers to purchase a book for every person in the room. If there are 100 people in attendance and you can sell your book for $15, you're probably going to make about $1,000 in profit and your book is reaching every person there. If you've done a good job of creating a great book that engages readers quickly, many of those folks are actually going to read the book and then they might tell other people.

5. **Affiliate Sales**

   Is there a product or service you recommend in your book? You can set up an affiliate relationship with that product or person and either include a link in your book or a link to a resource page on your book. These links are called "affiliate links." When someone buys through one of those links, based on your recommendation, you'll receive a referral fee or a commission.

   For example, we recommend Publisher Rocket for all your keyword and Amazon Ad research. We've already mentioned it several times because it is tools we use every day. To see what an affiliate link looks like visit: www.booklaunchers.com/kd-pRocket. If you buy the software from that link, we get a small referral fee for your purchase.

A quick note: Amazon does not permit affiliate linking to Amazon products in Kindle books. Also, don't link directly to Amazon at all in your book or you could find it getting kicked back by services like Apple Books or Draft2Digital because their bots are on Amazon patrol.

Also, it goes without saying but you should never set up affiliate relationships just to make money. You will damage the trust of your audience if you recommend something that you don't actually love and use.

6. **Different Formats**

   If you offer a variety of formats—large print (if it's appropriate for your audience), audiobook, e-book—and create companion workbooks or journals that are translated into other languages, you're going to get more income from the same book.

7. **A YouTube Channel**

   Your book is monetized marketing and so is YouTube. Sure, you won't roll in cash in the early days of your channel but YouTube will let you make money from content while you're building an audience that will buy other things from you—your book, consulting time, or a course. Once you have 1,000 subscribers, you can monetize your channel and promote products to sell. You also may find yourself getting sponsorships.

   YouTube also adds value to a website and business because of its audience and revenue generation. Thanks to the ongoing revenue and brand recognition from YouTube, I was able to sell my old business website and its YouTube channel after several years of inactivity.

REPURPOSING YOUR CONTENT

Eric Brotman wanted to write a book that reframed retirement as a kind of graduation. He didn't want people to see retirement as the end of their lives or careers; he wanted them to see it as the beginning. Through the development of his book, he ended up creating content that has become the foundation of a podcast, his website, articles for marketing, and a course. The concept of *Don't Retire! Graduate* is spreading everywhere because he has effectively repurposed his content.

Like Eric, you've also spent hours and hours figuring out how to explain the important concepts in your profession or your business for your book. You've hopefully developed clever ways to entertain and engage your audience with stories, acronyms, case studies, diagrams, anecdotes, and examples.

The good news is that all of that can be used in many different ways to help you further build your brand, promote your book, and boost your business. Hopefully, it will give your audience the feeling that you're everywhere with amazing material that they can use.

Content marketing is a valuable tool for selling your book, growing your business, and building your brand. With your book, you have some of the most refined and thought out content you'll ever have – it makes sense to use it over and over.

You see, you may know you've used that lesson from your book for a video, a podcast, an article, a Facebook post, and media interviews but your audience won't necessarily know that. Even if they do, they usually appreciate the reinforcement and repetition of good ideas or they skip on to the next one you have to offer.

Here are 10 ways to repurpose your book material to benefit you and your brand for the next year:

1. Find sections that are 500–1,000 words that can stand alone. You don't need to read any other parts of the book for it to make sense. You may box these sections out to stand alone in a book, but sometimes they are sections like this one, for ex-

ample, covering the five steps to accomplish something or the 10 ways to use your content. You can use them on your website, other websites, in magazine articles or other publications. Make a list and start to distribute them as you market your book and your business.

2. Shoot videos on each of the core subjects in your book. The content of subsections of your book could be produced as YouTube videos, while a chapter might provide content for a longer livestream or webinar. For example, a list like this could be turned into a single video (10 Ways to Repurpose Your Book Content) and each of the 10 points could be their own video. By breaking up your material or providing a few parts of a longer series, it's a great way to tease your book.

3. Choose at least one section in your book—possibly a chapter of your book—and turn it into a presentation for a webinar or before a live audience. It's important to prepare at least one talk (with a super clear benefit in it for the audience) if you have a self-help or business nonfiction book. It's quite likely you will be asked to speak, and it's a great opportunity for you to sell books and generate leads for your product or service. It's also an automatic credibility builder to be the one on stage!

4. Start a podcast based on the core theme of your book. You can either interview experts around the subjects in your chapters or do solo podcast episodes discussing your lessons and teachings.

5. Turn paragraphs with simple tips into social media posts. Depending on the length or the power of the tip, these can be Facebook, LinkedIn, or Instagram posts. You can even find designers on sites like Upwork or Fiverr that will take these tips and turn them into branded imagery for social media. If you want to see how we do this, connect with Book Launchers on Instagram. You'll see examples of our content and the content of our authors being used for social media posting.

6. Create an additional workbook or worksheets. The areas in the book where you ask questions or give your reader homework can offer perfect opportunities to create a workbook or a download option. If it's a workbook, you can give it for free as a download or sell it separately on Amazon. As a free download, it will help you build your email newsletter, which can be an invaluable way to build your business, sell more books, and generate revenue from your book.

7. Speaking of newsletters, your book's tips and steps are great topics for an email newsletter. You can directly pull content from your book to share in your newsletter if you aren't sure what else to write that week or month.

8. Each major idea or chapter could become the topic of a livestream video on Facebook, YouTube, Instagram, Twitch, or all of them if you're simulcasting. You could also use it to host a room or start a conversation on Clubhouse.

9. Any resource, book, service, or person you recommend in the book could be featured on a resource sheet and that could be another value-add download opportunity.

10. If you have statistics or graphics in your book, those can be turned into infographics, which make for highly shareable content or downloads.

Your book is an incredible opportunity to grow your brand, build your business, and generate income from a lot more than just book sales. Saying you're a bestseller is good for your ego but it doesn't always lead to the big bucks in your bank.

Make bank with your book by using it to leverage into bigger and better things.

LEVERAGE YOUR SPEAKING ENGAGEMENTS LIKE A BOSS

For years, I did a lot of speaking engagements that didn't pay me any fees. That's the real estate industry for you. But I was able to leverage those engagements to sell thousands of books and generate a lot of clients for my businesses.

I don't think many people realize how many speaking engagements are unpaid these days or even how many are pay-to-play; in other words, there are a crazy number of events where they charge speakers to take the stage. I've never paid to speak but knowing how valuable it can be to appear on the right stage, I understand why some speakers do it.

But before you get to that point, let's make sure your speaking opportunities either sell books or grow your platform. Your book will help you get the speaking opportunity but it's up to you to make the most of it.

Here's how I suggest you leverage speaking opportunities that don't pay:

- ✔ Promote your participation in newsletters, social media, and on your website. You're doing this for two reasons: 1) It boosts your credibility for others, and 2) organizers at the event will appreciate your helping them get the word out, and they may refer you to other events or give you other opportunities around their platform like video interviews, blog posts, shout outs, and reposts.
- ✔ Research, plan, and leverage media coverage of the event. Smart event planners, especially those who run larger, 100-plus person events, typically arrange some sort of media coverage around their event. Most media outlets don't run promotional stories about events. But if you have a human interest angle related to the event, you can

suggest a media interview to the organizers and get coverage for the event and for yourself.

✔ Hire a professional photographer to get photos of your talk to use in your media kit, on your website, and even on social media. This is a great credibility booster so it can be worth it to get a pro shooting pictures of you speaking to and engaging with a large audience.

✔ Film the talk or ask for video coverage. Ask the organizers if they're recording the event and if you can get a copy of the video. I've never been turned down. Sometimes they ask that I don't use it for public purposes but they understand that as a speaker, you need video footage to book other gigs and will almost always help you out, especially when you're unpaid.

✔ If you're unpaid, collect email addresses with a feedback form. Carol Cox, a fantastic speaking coach, gave me this suggestion and it was brilliant. Hand out a worksheet to go along with your talk and provide the audience with a feedback form on their seat or near where they enter or exit the room. On the feedback form, invite people to sign up for your newsletter. Event organizers will rarely get upset with this, and you'll likely get 50 percent or more of the room to give you their email address.

✔ Ask if you can set up a table at the back to sell books.

✔ Get testimonials from the organizer. Letters of reference are ideal but a great testimonial can really help too.

TAX DEDUCTIONS

Your time is not tax deductible but in most cases your expenses related to your book are. Boost your returns on your book by making smart choices that lead to tax deductions. Check with your accountant first. But generally, any expenses involved in writing your book are deductible, whether you buy software for editing and design work or you hire professionals that do it all for you.

This is an especially good thing to keep in mind when you're deciding whether to get another writer to help you or not. Sometimes the most important consideration is, "What is my return on time?" Can you get a higher return on your time if you write the entire book yourself or if you spent time elsewhere and take the tax deduction for hiring a writer to draft the majority of your book? It's something to consider.

Ultimately, doing anything just to breakeven isn't a great goal. The good news is that you can make money on so much more than book sales. Breakeven is the absolute bare minimum you should expect of your venture into self-publishing, if you're willing to do the work to make a great return.

CHAPTER 20:

LIVES ARE ABOUT TO CHANGE

It's not the end when your book is done. In fact, it's really just the beginning. The real work lies ahead of you and so does most of the fun of being an author.

My first book changed my life but it wasn't changed in an instant. My life shifted over time, from the day I decided to write my book through the months when I followed through and made it happen. When it launched and topped Amazon, my life still didn't transform in an instant. I did, however, begin moving into a new group of colleagues. I was now on stage with the experts I used to look up to. And authors with book deals reached out to get my help with their books. An entirely new world opened up to me one email and one phone call at a time.

The entire experience led me to reconnect with my first love—writing. It also unlocked, in my mind, a clear need in the market for full support self-publishing service. It took me awhile to picture what the ideal company would look like to serve authors who were just like me, but when I could see it, I started Book Launchers. For the first time in my life I feel like every experience, course, degree, and business I've had was to prepare me for building this business. I've never before felt so in alignment with what I am doing, who I work with, and how I want to serve others as I do in this moment. And it all began with my first book. And the crazy part is that building Book Launchers was never my goal when I published that first book. All I was thinking about was the real estate investors that needed my help and that I really wanted to write a book.

Starting something new is scary and challenging but it's also exciting. You may have a clear vision of what your book is going to do for your reader and for your life, but I hope you're open to the possibilities that are about to find you. The results of publishing a book are never just one thing and they never come all in one day.

That's why it's so important to invest in writing a book you'll be proud of for the rest of your life. Anything less than that is short changing your future self.

The good news is that you now have all the steps you need to write a great book—the next step is to go and do it! And, if you're done, well the work ahead to market your book is not small but it can be so fun. Here's where you actually get to help others with your hard work!

And before you worry about all the things you need to do to market your book, celebrate! You've done something that few people do: You've written a book. And if you followed the guidance in this book, you probably wrote a pretty fantastic one, and are prepared to put the full force of your intelligence and creativity behind it. (Be sure to visit me on YouTube at BookLaunchers.TV and tell me about it!)

Books change lives. I'm so excited for you and your readers and the impact your book will have on all of you.

ACKNOWLEDGEMENTS

While pregnant and unable to sleep through the night I spent all my extra time researching the publishing industry, working on the business plan for Book Launchers, and developing our service model. Once I launched the business, I was still up at 4:00 a.m. building the company because I was feeding and changing my new baby and unable to fall back asleep after. For that reason, I have to acknowledge my son, Jackson. The foundation of the company is incredibly solid and I can thank him for all that focus time he gave me to create the vision.

But, without Jaqueline Kyle and Tim Testa, the #noboringbooks philosophy and process would not exist today. When we started I gave them ten beta clients to work with, the vision of writing books with marketing in mind, and the requirement that our books would be as good or better quality than a traditionally published book. The truth is, I had no idea how to actually do that. I was a real estate investor who'd written a couple of books—I wasn't a publishing expert! They brought their enthusiasm, expertise, and experience to help me figure out how the heck we would actually do that! And what you've read in these pages are largely as a result of what we've built and learned together.

I also must thank my YouTube Besties and YouTube supporters (you know who you are because I give you regular shoutouts on BookLaunchers.TV), with a special shout out to Dale L. Roberts and Kevin Maguire. In the early days, when engagement on the channel was low, you two showed up to every live stream, commented on every video, and shared the channel. Every new YouTube channel should be so lucky as to have one or two folks like you to help them get the growth and momentum going.

I could go on because my husband and parents always deserve a shout out for anything and everything I accomplish, and there are plenty of clients who have helped us develop this process and many who've inspired and taught me along the way but it would be a great shame to end a #noboringbooks book with a boring acknowledgement. So…stop reading and start writing! Readers need you.

And, if you don't know where to start, please reach out to us for help. It's not only an honor, it's an absolute pleasure to help authors realize their dream of publishing a great book and get it into readers hands.

Visit: booklaunchers.com/bookacall to set up a call.

LET'S BUST BORING TOGETHER

For discounted bulk purchases of this book for your company, association, or conference, please email us at **team@booklaunchers.com**

To book Julie Broad for interviews or speaking visit **juliebroad.com** or contact **team@booklaunchers.com**

To Download Our *Gameplan to Sell 1000 Books*, visit **www.booklaunchers.com/gameplan**

For all other resources and support visit **www.booklaunchers.com**

in /BOOK-LAUNCHERS   🐦 @BOOKLAUNCHERS

📷 @BOOKLAUNCHERS   ▶ BOOKLAUNCHERS.TV

f /BOOKLAUNCHERS   🌐 BOOKLAUNCHERS.COM